ALTERNATIVE WEDDINGS

The essential guide for those
who want something different

JANE ROSS-MACDONALD

D0785159

Thorsons
An Imprint of HarperCollins*Publishers*

Thorsons
An Imprint of HarperCollins*Publishers*
77–85 Fulham Palace Road
Hammersmith, London W6 8JB
1160 Battery Street
San Francisco, California 94111–1213

Published by Thorsons 1996
10 9 8 7 6 5 4 3 2 1

A catalogue record for this book
is available from the British Library

ISBN 0 7225 3123 0

Printed in Great Britain by
HarperCollinsManufacturing Glasgow

CONTENTS

ACKNOWLEDGEMENTS

I would like to thank the following people who shared details of their weddings with me and gave permission for me to quote from their ceremonies (some of the names have been changed at their request):

Katy and Peter Clement, who married on a beach in Florida and had a non-denominational church blessing one year later;

Roz and Dave Morris, who married in a hotel room in Mexico City;

Robert and Miranda Holden, who had an open-air blessing drawing on a variety of spiritual traditions;

Sarah Carver and Paul Rees, who had a vegetarian reception in a Friends Meeting Hall after a register office ceremony;

Maria Coello and Stephen Newton, who conducted their own pacifist ceremony in a forest;

Alison Vickers and Tim Wainwright, who had a civil service followed by a ceremony of blessing and celebration in Alison's parents' garden;

James Clifton and Sharon Williams, who had a Pagan ceremony on top of Glastonbury Tor;

Nicola and Alasdair Saunders, who had a tenth-century Viking-style wedding;

Joanna Webb and Tony Moore, who married in a theatre in Australia;

Karen and Lee Chang-Rawlinson, who had a Pagan/lesbian ceremony in a friend's back garden;

Nicola and Pascal Lecerf, who married in the Seychelles on an astrologically auspicious day;

Margaret Gregory and Colin Wall, who had a civil service in the presence of their three-week-old son;

Philip and Steve Hawkesford-Curry, who had an evening ceremony based around an adaptation of the Humanist gay 'affirmation' ceremony;

Christine Baker and Mark Willis, who had a Humanist celebration outside the Peace Pagoda in Milton Keynes;

Christine Kijko, who married her partner, Jim, in hospital;

Roy Dalgleish and Martin Weaver, who had a celebration of partnership in a castle in the Forest of Dean;

Amanda Shribman and Avril Hollings, who held a lesbian commitment ceremony with Pagan, Goddess, Jewish and Buddhist elements;

Nicola and Humphrey Cobbold, whose wedding combined Jewish and Christian elements;

Janet and John Moorhouse, who held a Buddhist ceremony after a civil wedding;

Nahid Moshtael and Peter Gregory, who had a Baha'i wedding;

Diane Wilkinson and Simon Bebbington, who had a Humanist wedding in the grounds of Sheffield Polytechnic;

Darcy Twose and Peter Walop, who held a Humanist ceremony in the grounds of a hotel overlooking the sea at St Ives;

Catherine and Ian Beaumont, who married on a Hawaiian beach;

Sumita Davis and Stewart Maland, who had a Las Vegas wedding;

Jeanette and Jim Kelly, who married in the town hall in Prague.

I'd also like to thank the following people for their help while I was researching the different traditions and ceremonies in this book: George Broadhead, Richard Kirker, Carmen Henry, Sally Spears, the Rev. John Clifford and the Rev. Andrew Hill, Gyles Brandreth MP, Simon Allen, Lawrence Murray, Wendy Tennant and Mark Rimmer. Everyone at Thorsons (you all know who you are) but particularly Erica Smith for commissioning this book in the first place and Lisa Eaton for her tactful and professional editing. Finally I'd like to thank all the Ross-Macdonalds, Graham-Maws and Werrys for their unflagging support and occasional musical contributions.

I am indebted to the following for permission to reprint extracts:

Marriage Prayer (page 16) © Robert and Miranda Holden.
6 lines from *Weddings from the Heart* (page 52) © 1991,
Daphne Rose Kingma. Reprinted by permission of
Conari Press.
ASB Wedding Service (page 80ff) reprinted by permission of
the Central Board of Finance of the Church of England.
Spiritualist Wedding Ceremony (page 108ff) reprinted by permission of the Spiritualists' National Union.
Pagan Wedding Ritual (page 111ff) from *Rituals for Everyday Living* © 1994, Lorna St Aubyn. Reprinted by permission of Piatkus Books.
Druid Wedding (page 116ff) from *The Druid Way* © 1993,
Philip Carr-Gomm. Reprinted by permission of Element Books.
7 lines from *To Love and To Cherish* (page 126) © 1988, Jane Wynne Willson. Reprinted by permission of the author.
Gay and Lesbian Humanist Ceremony (page 139ff) reprinted by permission of GALHA.

FOR RUPERT

ABOUT THE AUTHOR

Jane Ross-Macdonald was educated in
London, Canterbury and Cambridge.
For the past ten years she has worked
in publishing, commissioning books on
alternative health, personal development, psychology and relationships. She
lives in Islington with her husband and
two cats.

PREFACE

ONGRATULATIONS!

Taking the decision to spend the rest of your life with someone is a major event in anyone's life. It might be something you have dreamt of ever since you were a small child reading fairy stories, it might be a long-waged campaign to capture the heart of a certain someone, or it might suddenly come upon you with the fierceness of a flash of lightning. For others it is a quieter, calmer sense of 'coming home'. It is a decision you make as a couple, together: gradually with a dawning sense of realization, or suddenly, passionately, inevitably.

Many couples feel the need to mark this rite of passage with a public celebration rather than drifting into long-term cohabitation and want the ceremony to express their love for each other in a meaningful way. Together, perhaps over dinner or walking along a beach, you discuss the kind of wedding you want. Some will opt for the traditional white church wedding, with all the trimmings. Those from different religious backgrounds may follow the traditional Jewish, Hindu or Muslim ceremony. Others choose the civil ceremony in a register office, with perhaps a family lunch afterwards.

For a growing number of couples, however, the decision is not so clear cut. If you are not strongly religious and feel a traditional wedding would be hypocritical, if you feel the civil ceremony is rather austere, if you have been married before or are marrying someone from a different culture, if you are gay or lesbian, if your two families are at loggerheads, or if your finances can't stretch to a lavish 'do'. . . in short, if you want a different, personal, meaningful wedding which expresses your own view of the world, what can you do?

This book aims to set out the options for creating your own wedding. It looks at various religious and spiritual traditions as well as non-religious weddings. It explains exactly what the legal issues are, and how much leeway you have in designing your own ceremony and choosing the venue. Covering all the stages, from proposal to honeymoon, it will give you ideas for writing your own vows, with sample services and real-life examples. It will also give you suggestions for readings, music and venues – whether you want to 'spice up' an otherwise traditional wedding, or go for a completely alternative one.

The possible range of alternative weddings is as rich and varied as your imagination, so inevitably this book does not try to be comprehensive. I hope it will, however, provide you with a good overview of a wide variety of different types of wedding and inspire you to make your own choices.

While I was researching this book, I talked to many couples who had chosen a different style of wedding. These ranged from two people who were married in a hotel room in Mexico having bribed some officials and dragged a couple of witnesses off the street, through couples who chose tropical islands for their weddings, to couples who wrote their own vows for ceremonies outside a temple or in a forest.

The most important piece of advice these couples offered is to *make your own decisions* and not to be deflected from doing what you want by parents, friends or relatives. Remember, it is *your* day, *your* wedding, the start of *your* lives together. Create a wedding that is special and sacred for you, that expresses your intentions, wishes and feelings, and you will find that it will be a joyous and romantic occasion to remember for the rest of your lives.

PART I

ONE

MARRIAGE IN THE 1990S AND BEYOND

O ver 300,000 couples in Britain tie the knot each year, undeterred by the escalating rate of divorce; evidence of, as Beatrice Webb noted, 'the triumph of hope over experience' or – less cynically – proof that romance is alive and well, and that people have a fundamental urge to declare their love for each other publicly and make a positive statement of enduring commitment.

These couples are bombarded with advice, magazines, mail-shots, books, exhibitions – one huge industry with the sole aim of 'making your special day a day to remember', thereby making handsome profits for dressmakers, cake decorators, printers, florists, gift shops, caterers and a host of others. Every wedding magazine exhorts young brides to buy into the myth of a perfect white wedding, offering 'essential' advice on what to wear, what not to wear, how many ushers to have, colour schemes, bridesmaids' shoes, long lasting make-up, timing, seating plans ... implying that any departure from the norm would be a dreadful faux pas. It is hardly surprising, then, that it can take up to a year to organize a large traditional wedding – a year that can at best be frenetically busy, at worst fraught with heated rows, tears, and threats to call it all off.

Stephen (29, a bond dealer) talks of how he was completely excluded from the wedding arrangements by his bride's mother:

She insisted on doing it all herself. Flowers, food, guest list, the lot. She even chose the hymns! I should have been more assertive, I suppose, but I didn't want to cause a fuss. And at first I was pleased not to have to bother with all the details. Suzanne seemed quite happy with the situation but it did cause problems between the two of us in the run-up to the wedding and we'd have endless arguments about the tiniest things.

Elizabeth (25, an actress) had divorced parents. Her father had a new wife and stepchildren and her mother had just divorced from her second husband:

You wouldn't believe the rows we had over the wording of the invitations. I wanted both my parents to be on it, my mother wanted to use her maiden name and my father didn't want her on it at all! Both wanted the replies to come to them. In the end we had to get two sets printed. Alan and I felt we should have been given awards for services to diplomacy after six months of careful negotiating with each set of parents!

Unless you are very careful, there are so many things that can conspire against the two most important people, the bride and groom. Instead of your wedding being a special, personal event, it becomes a public pageant of inestimable cost, complicated by an assortment of friends and relatives offering well-meant but intrusive advice. As Vivienne (33, a fashion journalist) said:

By the time we got to the wedding day itself, we had almost forgotten why we were doing it. I consider myself a sensible, well-adjusted, thoughtful person, but even I became consumed by worries about buttonholes, royal icing and marquee swags. It wasn't until our quiet honeymoon on the Isle of Skye that we felt *really* married, in the spiritual sense.

Clara (22, a secretary), who was planning a traditional white wedding – huge train, marquee, 200 guests at the church ('the works') – described her reaction after seeing the film *Four Weddings and a Funeral*:

> I can't see why everyone thought it was such a hilarious film. It felt like my plans for a dream wedding had been ripped to shreds. It made me see how boring and how samey church weddings are. Now I'm determined to do something different, even if it's only having a twenties theme, chocolate cake and leaving by hot-air balloon!

These are, if you like, the negative reasons for not going down the aisle in white. But quite apart from the fuss and bother of a traditional wedding, couples are starting to want to do things their own way. No longer feeling straight-jacketed by convention, pulling away from organized religion and experimenting with new ideas, people are searching out their own directions. Ostentation is out, simplicity is in, as the materialism of the 1980s gives way to a new individuality and sense of spirituality. Marriage is not socially essential these days, so people are thinking very carefully about why they are doing it and what it means for them. The very idea of marriage is changing, just as it has evolved through several incarnations over thousands of years. If you are considering doing it differently you are at the cutting edge of this trend!

In such a climate you may be forgiven for wondering why it took so long to change the laws that decreed (prior to 1995) that the only alternative to a church wedding was the register office serving your own area. We have Gyles Brandreth, MP for Chester, to thank for introducing much-needed changes to the Marriage Act. We can now pick and choose our register office or marry in a licensed hotel, stately home or other 'suitable' venue:

> As an enthusiastic advocate of marriage, I want to do away with unnecessary restrictions on where people can marry . . . for some couples a register office may not be the ideal setting for their

wedding. They may want to have more guests than the register office can accommodate. They may want a more stylish and memorable setting for a ceremony that is of unique importance in any couple's life . . . I hope my Bill will enable more couples to celebrate their marriages in the place and manner of their choosing.

Gyles Brandreth, 1994

The law is still somewhat restrictive (as you will discover on page 22), but there are creative ways to do things while remaining within the law. Even before the law changed, I discovered couples who had challenged the status quo and found wonderful alternatives to the church versus register office options. Although no other country has quite reached the excesses of the US, where weird and wonderful weddings have been commonplace for years, we are beginning to see some genuinely different weddings in this country.

What exactly is it that prompts couples to choose their own way? Here are some reasons I came across from speaking to the people who contributed to this book.

PATRIARCHAL AND SEXIST SYMBOLISM

Quite apart from the fervent wish of most modern brides never to utter the word 'obey' as part of their wedding vows, the entire church ceremony is charged with overtones which many women, and increasingly men, find hard to reconcile with their lifestyles and attitudes. The woman, dressed in virginal white, modestly veiled, is handed over by her father or another male to her new husband. Things are done *to* her, rather than *by* her: 'I didn't want to be given away – I'm not a parcel!' commented Katy (21, a student). The emphasis is also on the procreation of children, whether you want to have them or not – whether you are able to have them or not:

I didn't want such a personally important occasion to be put in a religious context (with its 'marriage is created by God for the creation of children' business) when what was important was that I

6

was making a commitment to a person.

Roz (27, a journalist)

THE NEED TO PERSONALIZE THE SERVICE

When you stand up to make your vows before witnesses, you want to convey your feelings truly and sincerely – your signature needs to be on the whole day. The couples I spoke to wanted the service to express who they were and why they were marrying. Many wanted to say more than was possible with the standard wedding service, and to make it more personal. 'Your wedding day is the most authentic day of your life. If you aren't true to yourself then when can you be?' asked Robert (25, a writer and psychologist), while Sarah (26, a social worker) and Paul (29, a child psychiatrist) felt, 'We didn't want to be hypocrites on such an important day (or ever!)'

Maria (25, a teacher) and Stephen (24, a teacher), who devised their own ceremony and held it in a forest, wanted their wedding to be:

A celebration of the type of people we are, so it was important that our common beliefs and values were a part of that celebration. If we'd had a traditional wedding it would not have said anything about our relationship with each other.

Decide what values you want your wedding to embody, and you will find the service will fall into place. Said Alison (29, campaigns director for Amnesty International):

We wanted a wedding which both we and our friends felt comfortable with. We were committed to a ceremony in which we played equal roles, and which could have been equally relevant to our gay friends. We wanted to get married in a beautiful place (my parents' garden) and have a sense of space and light and celebration.

Weddings certainly can be dull. One summer I went to nine traditional church weddings. They have all now merged in my mind – a fact which I put down to the similarity of the proceedings rather than the quantity of champagne I consumed. Roz and Dave (35, an author), who married in Mexico, insisted: 'We wanted a personal, unique wedding, not a rerun of a ceremony everyone has seen hundreds of times.'

A DESIRE FOR CELEBRATION
AND ROMANCE OVER SOLEMNITY

Traditional services can sometimes be over-formal, sacrificing joy and romance at the altar of respectability. By creating your own ceremony and choosing where to get married – whether it be a beautiful European city or in a canoe in the Lake District – you can inject enthusiasm and happiness without feeling boring and conventional. After all, you will (ideally) never get married again, so you might as well make sure you have fun on the day. James (25, a hairdresser) and Sharon (29, a Reiki Master and therapist), who met on an ashram in Goa, opted for a non-legal ceremony on Glastonbury Tor: 'A lot of people are put off by marriage itself. It wasn't that we particularly wanted not to conform, but we felt religious weddings were too fanatical and didn't convey enough love.'

> As we were in America and visa problems meant we had to return to the UK, we simply decided that a Las Vegas wedding would be the most exciting way to end our time in the US and would help us return with happy memories.
>
> *Sumita (24, an administrator)*

SPIRITUALITY AS OPPOSED TO CHRISTIANITY

I spoke to several couples who firmly assured me that they were deeply spiritual people but who nevertheless could not find anything in Christianity that answered their needs or reflected their beliefs in a meaningful way. These are the people who refused to compromise with a church wedding, despite the temptations of solemnity and grandeur.

> Neither of us assigns ourself to a particular denomination or its inherent values. However we do believe in some type of universal power. We wanted our celebration to include the essence of marriage from all faiths, for every faith seems to teach that what you give out you get back. Having both experienced multi-culturalism in different ways in our lives, we wanted everyone to feel comfortable at our wedding, no matter what their faith or background.
>
> *Maria and Stephen*

'Neither of us has any religious or spiritual convictions,' said Nicola (27, a technical writer) and Alasdair (26, a civil servant), 'and we are both fascinated by Viking society.' Naturally enough, their ceremony was designed according to a tenth-century Viking ceremony.

Joanna (29, an actress) and Tony (42, a theatre director and technician) met at a play rehearsal and ended up running a theatre in Australia together: the natural venue for their wedding. Tony has Buddhist leanings and Joanna is agnostic and partially psychic. A friend who was a Uniting Church chaplain offered to be the celebrant.

Other couples felt free to follow their own beliefs. Lee (33, a retailer) and Karen (31, a student) designed a Pagan ceremony with elements of Buddhism and made it relevant to each of them. Apala (25, a journalist) and Julian (33, a publishing manager) searched long and hard for an open-air ceremony that reflected both her lapsed Catholic belief in God and angels and his passionate agnosticism. In the end they settled for a civil service followed by a ceremony conducted by an Anglican vicar with 'the imagination to share a God for all people'. With opposition from her mother, she comments sadly: 'An in-between ceremony like ours falls into the abyss of the illegitimate, the irreverent, the forbidden; not just for my mother, but also for the civil and religious authorities in this country.' (*Guardian*, 13 July 1994)

CHRISTIANITY AS OPPOSED TO 'CHURCHIANITY'

Robert and Miranda (25, a writer and healer) felt that Christianity *did* have much to offer for them. They discovered, however, that the vicar of the church they wanted to marry in (which was at the bottom of Robert's grandmother's garden) insisted they live in the parish for six months instead of what was in fact five months and three weeks before the date they had chosen! In the end, this ridiculous red tape led them to drop the church wedding in favour of a civil marriage followed by a ceremony in the garden.

A DESIRE FOR SIMPLICITY

At its heart, a marriage is about two people committing themselves to each other for life. That is all. It is a big deal, but it's also a remarkably profound, intimate and simple act, and it is quite understandable that you may not want to clutter it up with traditional trappings. As one couple said:

> We felt that church weddings seem to detract from the couple marrying. It's mainly for social acceptance and respectability, and to please family, relatives and friends whom you never see at any other time. And they are so expensive!

MIXED MARRIAGES

It is becoming more and more common for couples from different countries, cultures, religions and ethnic backgrounds to want to marry. Some religions are extremely strict and will not allow this; others are more flexible. The best way of combining the two is to pull elements of each together in a new unique ceremony, with two celebrants – one from each side – to officiate.

FAMILY PROBLEMS

If you have what sociologists today call a 'blended' family, chances are not everyone will get on. Even without a proliferation of ex-wives, stepfathers or half-siblings, weddings do tend to bring together parts of the family that are sometimes best separated. People are usually able to bury their differences for the sake of the couple marrying, although even in the most placid of families the run-up to a wedding can be traumatic and full of heated arguments. If your families cannot be safely gathered together, you might want to escape to a palm-fringed beach or have a quickie wedding in Las Vegas while on holiday. As Neil Hamilton (a transport manager) and Patricia Tierney (35, a charity worker) said: 'We decided to get married in Sarajevo because there's something special about the place, and because it's the only place our families couldn't come, and we wanted a quiet wedding.' (*Daily Telegraph*, 26 August 1994)

If you come from a home with a different set-up from the traditional (though no longer common) nuclear family, you may also find the established wording of a traditional ceremony abrasive and inappropriate.

SECOND MARRIAGES

If either of you is marrying for the second or third time around, you will of course want to do it differently. A church wedding may not be possible (it is usually up to the discretion of the vicar) and you would be forgiven for not wanting to repeat the exact vows you spoke years before with someone else. A Seychelles wedding was an ideal choice for one couple I interviewed. As Nicola (31, a dentist) said:

Pascal was divorced and neither of us are regular churchgoers so it didn't seem important to have the church sanctify our union. We didn't want to have to make a choice between a wedding in France or England. We fixed the date and time in consultation with an astrologer who studied our natal charts. In fact as we signed the Register a double rainbow appeared in the sky behind us.

They obviously made the right choice!

PRACTICAL CONSIDERATIONS

Space, time, money . . . if you haven't got the luxury of an abundance of all three you will probably need to depart from the traditional formula. A white wedding 'with all the trimmings' can cost thousands of pounds. So can a non-traditional wedding, of course, but with fewer conventions to meet, you will find the cost drops dramatically. Weddings combined with honeymoons, for example, weddings in your garden at home, weddings abroad. Simple, moving weddings with a few friends.

> We are atheists and our wedding was arranged on impulse, a decision made when we knew that our families would be spending Easter with us. We also had a very limited income at the time and had just had a baby – really we wanted the minimum of fuss.
>
> *Margaret (25, a mental health care manager)*
> *and Colin (24, a chartered accountant)*

GAY AND LESBIAN COUPLES

Gay couples cannot legally marry in this country. Indeed, the Church publicly rejects the practice of homosexuality. Apart from the legal issues, all the above reasons apply of course to gay and lesbian couples. Martin (28, a sexual health officer) and Roy (27, a computer programmer) explained that one of them was a Spiritualist and the other a lapsed Catholic. They wanted a commitment ceremony that came from them, which reflected who they were – and made a statement to friends and family. Another couple, Philip (34, a local government officer) and Steve (28, a chef), said they were both spiritual, although Philip was basically agnostic, while Steve was originally from a Baptist background but had stopped going to church due to what he saw as hypocrisy. They wanted their ceremony to bear as little resemblance to a heterosexual wedding as possible – to make their own statement and keep the seriousness of the occasion paramount.

RENEWING YOUR VOWS

Couples are increasingly choosing to renew their vows, perhaps on a significant anniversary. This is a chance to have a public affirmation of your relationship and the values by which you have been living. Barbara Taylor Bradford renewed her vows during a second honeymoon in Antigua.

Although you may prefer not to replicate too many of the details of your original wedding, for the structure of the ceremony you may follow the format of one of the ceremonies in this book, adapting and altering it as appropriate. The officiant will offer help and advice, but keep it simple and warm.

⑥

Of course, in practice what drives couples to create their own alternative wedding is a combination of all of these reasons. For couples who think carefully about the kind of wedding they want, it seems to become increasingly impossible to opt for the traditional format, unless of course they are committed to a certain faith. Christine (42, a writer and relationships psychologist) and Mark (35, an educational publisher) chose their wedding for several reasons:

> We wanted a ceremony that truly reflected who we were, and was therefore largely designed and determined by us and to our criteria. We wanted a ritual that marked a rite of passage, and could not find one that reflected our beliefs honestly. We wanted a ceremony that fully involved all those there in a very practical way.

Taking the decision *not* to have a traditional church wedding does not automatically mean that the preparations running up to the day and dealings with your families will run completely smoothly. In some ways there are more initial difficulties to be overcome. However, with careful planning and a firm overarching belief in the kind of wedding you both want, you may feel surprisingly free. Untrammelled by convention, you can simply get on with organizing the kind of day you want. Deciding to branch out and do your own thing can be a scary and isolating experience. It can also be incredibly liberating and exciting. This book will help you plan a stylish, original and imaginative wedding, no matter what your beliefs.

I'd like to close this chapter with a caveat. Don't let your *wedding day* detract from your *marriage*. One is a celebration of the other. Your wedding day is undeniably an amazingly special one, but it is not the be-all and end-all, so do not focus all your energies just on one day. In fact your wedding day is the beginning, just one of thousands of days you will hopefully be together. Start your married life together as you mean to go on: making decisions and choices as a couple.

ALTERNATIVE PROPOSALS

Before we move on to weddings themselves, you might like to consider different ways of asking your partner for their 'hand in marriage'. Even in these days of sexual equality, it is still fairly unusual for the woman to propose, but why wait for a leap year? Take a leaf out of the book of girls from the Trobriand Islands of Papua New Guinea, who approach their desired mate and bite him! For couples who have been together for years, there may be no need even for one to propose to the other: you may have a mutual understanding that you want to spend your lives together and the wedding day becomes a practical, rather than a romantic decision.

Traditionally proposals are made over dinner or while on holiday, at Christmas, on Valentine's Day or on birthdays. I know people who live on tenterhooks from special occasion to special occasion, wondering when The Question might be popped, or waiting anxiously for the most 'romantic' moment to propose. What could be less spontaneous? If you want to avoid the clichés, choose a moment when they are least expecting it: in the bath, in the middle of an argument, in the fast lane of a motorway? Or send a surprise bunch of flowers with a note, leave a proposal on their pillow for them to find if you are away on business, or get a DJ to read it out on the radio. If you like grand, theatrical gestures, you could organize a fire-writing display to light up 'Will you marry me?' in fireworks, or book a poster site on your partner's way home from work (contact Adshel, who can usually arrange this unless you want a very popular site – you print the poster, they stick it up, and a week's space will cost you a few hundred pounds). You could even get an aeroplane to trail a message through the sky (contact your local general aviation airfield, who will let you know if it is something they can arrange).

The most unusual words used for a proposal that I came across were from a young man who, after years of pressure to get engaged, said to his girlfriend: 'Well, shall we inform your parents of the imminent change in our cohabitational status then?' These were not words from the heart, and the wedding was cancelled two weeks before it was due to take place.

If what you want is a wedding from the heart, read on.

MARRIAGE PRAYER

During the time that you are engaged, try not to forget what you are doing and why you are doing it. Marriage is one of the deepest rites of passages we experience and offers feelings we must hold on to.

You might like to recite the following prayer – written by Robert and Miranda Holden – each day or each week leading up to your wedding, in order to prepare yourselves mentally for the life-enhancing event ahead:

Oh Divine Creator of all this Wonder,
We stand before you with our hearts and minds
open and ready to receive Your Divine
Inspiration, Clarity and Truth in order
to create a beautiful, joyful and
inspiring ceremony for our marriage.

We devote our union to You and thank You
infinitely for bringing us together.
May our marriage and all of our wedding
plans be blessed and inspired by You,
so that we can get closer to You in
order to unfold into our Highest
Purpose on Earth.

May this unfoldment bring love and joy
to all those we meet, and may we have the
privilege of acting as channels
through which Your Divine Light may
enter the world.
SO BE IT.

TWO

MARRIAGE
AND THE LAW

⟨⟩

Marriage is a binding together of a man and woman to live in an indivisible union.

Emperor Justinian

P lanning a wedding is romantic and exciting: the air is charged with promises made, and more to be made; you are the toast of your friends and relatives; you are making plans for your life together. It can also be a manically busy time, depending on the scale of the wedding you are planning, the time you have, and the extent to which you are having to cope with relatives who may disagree with the type of wedding you have chosen. It is easy to forget at such a time that marriage is, at its most basic, a legal agreement. Indeed, if you are intending to have a non-church wedding, or want to know what your options for a civil wedding are, you need to be crystal clear on where you stand. Of course, you may decide not to have a legally recognized wedding at all.

Marriage has been variously described as a civil contract, a status and an institution. It has been around for thousands of years, and what to us is a traditional Christian wedding is, in fact, relatively new. Originally invented to promote the stability of society and for the protection of women and children, marriage has far-reaching effects on both family and social relationships, and carries with it rights and obligations: to children, property and to each other.

GETTING MARRIED IN THE UK: A QUICK GUIDE TO THE LAW

In England and Wales, you cannot get married if:

- either of you is under 16
- either of you is under 18 and does not have parental consent
- either of you is already married
- a previous wife or husband of either of you has been missing for less than seven years (at seven years they may be presumed dead, but this is a complex area of the law) or you do not have a certificate of divorce based on presumption of death
- you are closely related
- you are not both sane and sober at the time of the wedding

A legal marriage can be solemnized in several different ways:

CHURCH MARRIAGES

MARRIAGE BY BANNS

This is the standard procedure taken by those opting for a church wedding. You will need to give the minister all your personal details. Reading of the banns involves quaint terms such as 'spinster'. The aim is to publicize the wedding and to alert the minister to any 'just impediment'. Banns are read at both partners' local parish churches and must read on three successive Sundays before the wedding.

MARRIAGE BY SPECIAL LICENCE
GRANTED BY THE ARCHBISHOP OF CANTERBURY

This is needed if you are intending to get married in a church somewhere other than your own parish. Banns do not need to be read and the marriage can take place at any time. The alternative is to get yourself on the electoral role of that church. The vicar will tell you how this is done.

MARRIAGE BY COMMON LICENCE

If you want to get married quickly and dispense with the banns, a licence may be issued by the local diocesan council. Its purpose is to identify you as who you say you are, but you do need to get married within three months of its being issued.

CIVIL WEDDINGS

This is by far the most common form for people who do not wish to have a church marriage. The certificate can also be used when the marriage is in church, as long as the minister is happy for the ceremony to take place. If it does take place in a church a clergyman needs to officiate.

This provision was first introduced in 1836 in order to legalize marriages made by 'civil contract at a register office without any religious ceremony, and marriages in a registered building', other than a church or chapel of the Church of England (i.e. Nonconformist and RC marriages). Subsequently the registrar was empowered to give a certificate on the strength of which marriages could be solemnized according to the usages of the Society of Friends (Quakers), Jews and other religions. Many people, especially those marrying for a second time, choose to follow a civil service with a blessing in a church.

Just over half the marriages in Britain take place in a register office. The marriage needs to be solemnized with open doors (in order to admit any persons declaring any just impediment!) and in the presence of the Superintendent Registrar, the registrar, the couple and a minimum of two witnesses.

A civil marriage is either by certificate or by licence. You must give due notice in your own district and the following restrictions apply:

- To marry by certificate *without* licence both of you need to have been resident in a district in England or Wales for seven days immediately before giving the notice of marriage. If you live in different districts, notice of marriage must be given in both. The certificate which enables the marriage to proceed can be issued a minimum of 21 clear days after the notice has been given.
- To marry by certificate *and* licence only one of you needs to have lived in a district in England or Wales for 15 days before notice is given, while the other must be in a district in England or Wales on the day notice is given. The licence which enables the marriage to proceed can be issued after one clear day.

Both documents are valid for three months from the date on which notice of marriage is given, and the ceremony can take place in any register office or suitable alternative licensed venue in England or Wales. The following stipulations also apply:

- Public declaration – the couple must declare no lawful impediment according to the special formula, and they must follow the statutory form of verbal contract (*see* page 88).
- Witnesses – you must have two witnesses over the age of 18.
- Hours – Between 8 a.m. and 6 p.m., although a marriage outside these hours is not void. Chester Register Office recently hit the headlines when it became the first in the country to conduct a marriage service on a Saturday afternoon (rather than morning). If you wish to get married at dawn or at midnight, for example, you will need a special licence, unless you are Jewish or a Quaker. Register offices are closed on Sundays and some other times, so it is best to check.

SCOTLAND

The rules are more lax north of the border. In Scotland, for example, you can marry in any church you wish. You do not need parental consent if you are 16 or over (which is why lovers still arrive in their droves at Gretna Green, the first stop over the border) and you do not need to be resident in Scotland. You do need to apply for a Marriage Schedule by giving notice to the local registrar where you want to marry at least 15 days (but no longer than 3 months) beforehand, but banns are no longer legally required. The location and details of the Church of Scotland ceremony are entirely at the discretion of the minister. You can marry anywhere, at home or in a hotel, for example, or even outside, as long as the celebrant is registered. Second time around weddings in a church are also rarely a problem. What is important in the eyes of the law in Scotland is the celebrant, not the building. Any non-civil ceremony is classed as a religious ceremony, so if you choose this option you should apply to the Register General if you are unsure whether your faith is one of the official listed religions. The Humanists are not yet on this list, although they are having ongoing discussions.

There are no specific legal wording requirements in Scotland other than that the couple (who must be of different sexes and over 16) make a statement to the effect that they are taking each other as husband and wife, and that the celebrant should announce that they be husband and wife. The couple, the celebrant and two witnesses sign the Marriage Schedule, which is later given to the registrar who will fill in the Marriage Register.

NORTHERN IRELAND

Marriages in Northern Ireland take place either in a register office or church. The recent changes to the Marriage Act do not cover Northern Ireland.

WHERE CAN I MARRY?

Since the law has changed you can shop around for a register office: it needn't be the one nearest your home. In addition the new Act allows for certain venues to be licensed to hold civil weddings. Legally, the only proviso is that marriages must be conducted on 'approved premises'. According to the Office of Population, Censuses and Surveys, these approved premises must also be 'suitably solemn', although this is not specified in the Act itself. This opens up many possibilities for wedding locations, but the most likely venues are going to be hotels, stately homes and perhaps museums – provided the local authority has granted them a licence.

To be eligible for a licence a location must be accessible to the public, a permanent structure and, as mentioned above, suitably solemn, and licences will only be granted to actual buildings or (under special circumstances) moored boats. Hot-air balloons, aeroplanes, mountain tops and back gardens are definitely out, as is any building with any religious significance – at least for the moment. And sadly, the beautiful Isles of Scilly have been omitted from this section of the Act for the moment, due to a bureaucratic oversight. One suspects that, with the relaxing of the laws, authorities will find it increasingly difficult *not* to grant licences for unusual places: I heard on the radio recently that a motorway service station was applying for a licence! Be aware, though, that there is one less welcome aspect of the new Act: passers-by retain the right to attend marriage services, so be warned if you are holding a lavish reception. And if you want to marry somewhere other than in approved premises, you will have to go through a civil ceremony separately.

Applications must be advertised in local newspapers, allowing 21 days for objections to be made, and licences will be granted for an initial period of three years. The service has to be conducted by the registrar, but providing legal requirements are fulfilled, you can make it as personal as you like – as long as it is not religious.

This change in the law has been welcomed on all sides – apart, that is, from Barbara Cartland, doyenne of over-the-top traditional romanticism, who said on GLR (15 April 1995):

> I believe in romance. A Church wedding contains the hope that you'll have children, and the hope that you'll be together for ever. In this day and age you need every help you can get – and that comes from God.

Some local councils (such as Brent, which won the Government's Charter Mark Award in 1993 for excellence in public service) try to make the register office ceremony as personal and memorable as possible, allowing flowers, attendants, music and non-religious readings, and extending opening hours through Saturday afternoons.

Many couples take a very understated approach to the legal ceremony in the register office. Christine says:

> The registrar and her assistant were totally taken aback by our low-key approach and kept having to reassure themselves that we were 'having a blessing' at some point. We kept telling them that we weren't having a blessing because we weren't religious, and the low-key approach was deliberate because it wasn't the real ceremony, just a legal formality. Sunday was the real wedding and we wanted to make the distinction between the two events as clear and obvious in our minds – and everyone else's minds – as possible. We didn't even tell those invited to the wedding exactly when the registry office bit had been, but we're still a little miffed that our marriage certificate gives the date of the registry office bit, not the date of the 'real' wedding.

QUAKER WEDDINGS

Weddings are not subject to the timing rule (i.e. that they have to take place between certain hours of the day) and don't have to be in a registered building, office or church. You do not need to be a member of the Religious Society of Friends, but you must show a certificate signed by a registering officer of the Quakers to the effect that if either partner is not a member or of the persuasion they are authorized to get married. The ceremony is very simple, having changed very little since the seventeenth century (*see* page 84).

JEWISH WEDDINGS

Jewish weddings are both religious and civil. You must obtain a Superintendent Registrar's certificate or licence and deliver it to the secretary of the synagogue of which the groom is a member. You also need to apply to the religious authority under which the ceremony is taking place. Remember to take your documents (such as birth certificates and parents' Jewish marriage lines – you must both be members of the Jewish faith) and a witness, preferably a parent. Jewish weddings usually take place in a synagogue, but they are valid so long as they are under a *chuppah* (canopy). No further stipulation is made on the form of the marriage. Jewish people may also be married in the normal way before a registrar.

SECOND MARRIAGES

At the moment, divorcees are at the mercy of their parish priest if they wish to marry in church. They have no automatic right to do so, which does seem unfair when non-churchgoing couples marrying for the first time may easily arrange a religious wedding. However, perhaps in the knowledge that more people are searching for an alternative to the register office, a motion has been tabled at the Church of England's General Synod that would give divorced couples the right to a church wedding.

NONCONFORMIST OR FREE CHURCH WEDDINGS

To marry in a nonconformist church, notice must be given in the district where you live by certificate or licence, but banns are not necessary. You can only be married in the district where you live unless the church you wish to marry in is the usual place of religious worship for one or both of you, or there is no church of the required denomination in the district where one of you lives. A civil registrar must also be present, unless an authorized person has been appointed by the governing body of the Church. (*See* page 86 on Unitarian Weddings.)

ROMAN CATHOLIC MARRIAGES

You will need dispensation from the Catholic Church if you want to marry a non-Catholic in church. This will be given by the parish priest, providing you undertake to bring up any children according to the Catholic faith. Couples in the Republic of Ireland may marry in an RC ceremony outside a church at the discretion of their priest.

ORTHODOX CHURCHES

These churches include Bulgarian, Greek, Cypriot, Russian and Serbian. The ceremonies are rich in tradition, ritual and symbolism. Contact the authorities for each church direct if you are considering marrying in an orthodox church. They will be quite specific about their requirements.

GAY AND LESBIAN CEREMONIES

Homosexual 'marriages' are illegal in the UK. You could consider marrying in the Netherlands or in Norway, where 'registered partnerships' are legally accepted. The only legally recognized step in the UK is to change your names by deed poll, which a solicitor will arrange for you.

GETTING MARRIED ABROAD

In many countries marriages must be registered separately with the civil authorities. The UK is unusual in that churches have the right to carry out legal marriages.

The main thing to remember is that the law of the country prevails. Two witnesses are required plus the 'marriage officer', the marriage needs to be registered and copies of the entries should be sent to the Registrar General. On board a ship the marriage can be performed by a chaplain, officer or other person acting officially under the orders of the commanding officer of a British Army serving abroad.

The law varies from country to country, but you will probably need to check whether you should take:

- birth certificates (plus copies)
- letters stating you are employed in the UK (plus copies)
- a decree nisi, if either of you is divorced
- proof of single status
- passport photos
- translations of the above documents
- a certificate of 'non-impediment' (your local register office will provide this in the UK if you take in your birth certificates, but it will take 21 days)

When you are there you may need to:

- place a notice in a local newspaper asking for declarations of any just impediment
- post banns for a required number of days
- find two witnesses (although you could just pluck them from the street)
- hire a translator
- have a blood test (it is often possible to have these on the morning of your wedding)
- have a chest X-ray

- spend a few days in the country before marrying

The time you will have to spend there before you can marry varies from country to country. Curiously enough, EC countries can be the most problematic for non-indigenous couples wishing to marry. In Italy, for example, you will need to stay in the country for six weeks. In America, conditions vary from state to state (in Las Vegas, Florida and the Cayman Islands you can get spliced immediately), and in the Caribbean they vary from island to island. Barbados, for example, requires one day's residence, St Lucia two days' residence plus three days' paperwork. Antigua, Thailand, Jamaica, St Kitts, St Vincent and the British Virgin Islands all require three days' residence. For Bali you will have to be resident for seven days, plus a day in Jakarta to deal with the paperwork. Don't forget that there will be a fee, which again differs from country to country.

If you want to be clear about what the requirements are for the country you have chosen, phone the Foreign and Commonwealth Office or the relevant Embassy in London, stating your intention to marry in the specific country. They will advise you of the correct procedures. Alternatively, if you are going on a wedding/honeymoon package, the tour company will have all the answers and will usually fix all the legal niceties for you.

Remember, you may be dealing with a language you don't understand and may have trouble getting through the red tape. It could take longer to organize than you think.

If you marry abroad your wedding will not be registered in the UK, but it will be legally recognized. You may lodge a copy of your certificate and a translation with the Foreign Office, who could provide copies if they are needed.

THE LEGAL
IMPLICATIONS OF MARRIAGE

Being married gives you certain rights and protection in the case of separation, divorce or the death of your partner. If you decide not to have a legal marriage, it is worth bearing in mind the following (but remember that the laws governing marriage change regularly):

- There is no law governing the division of property should you separate. You would need to get a solicitor to draw up an agreement to cover a potential future separation.
- Your partner will not automatically inherit your estate should you die without a will. Again, go to a solicitor to draw up a will leaving property and possessions to specified parties. You could also take out an insurance policy and cite your partner as next of kin.
- Leaving anything to a non-married partner after your death will cause your partner to be liable to tax. Avoid this by making gifts during your lifetime.
- There is no legislation to cover children from cohabitees, apart from the right of a single mother to apply for a court order to cover maintenance for the child's upkeep from the father. Take legal advice about drawing up an agreement to cater for any eventuality.

CHANGING YOUR NAME

It is no longer the norm for women automatically to take on their husband's surname (it is not a legal necessity), and it is not unknown for the man to change his name to his wife's. Gay couples often hyphenate their names, the one legally recognized step in this country.

If you do decide to change your name, you will need to send a copy of your marriage certificate to any relevant official bodies in order to ask them to change their records and issue you with new documents. Bear in mind the following:

- car registration
- driving licence
- passport
- motoring organisation
- insurance policies
- pension plans
- building society
- bank for cheque book and cards
- credit card companies
- accounts department at work

If you do not have a marriage certificate, a solicitor can arrange for your names to be changed legally and will issue a certificate accordingly.

Some people, on changing their name, send out a card to friends and business associates announcing the fact that following their marriage to X on (date) they will be known as X.

To obtain a copy of the current Marriage Act, contact HMSO (Her Majesty's Stationery Office).

THREE

THE
IMPORTANT DAY . . .

⑥

Although you have decided you do not want a tradition-al white wedding, it is important for you and your guests to take the wedding seriously. You need to 'feel married' afterwards. For this reason there are ritual-istic, social and cultural elements you might want to include in order to add 'gravitas' to the proceedings. Make your selection from the following list:

- a sacred, beautiful or unusual setting
- a celebrant
- formal invitations
- special clothes for the bride, groom and guests
- a best man, bridesmaids or supporters
- arrival and 'handing over' from one family to another
- a circular format
- flowers
- music
- readings
- prayers
- vows
- exchange of rings
- a receiving line
- a post-wedding meal
- cake
- speeches

- singing and dancing
- confetti and 'going away'
- wedding gifts
- special touches
- a post-wedding trip

It is not the intention of this book to prescribe what you should or should not do, nor how far ahead of the 'big day' each element should be booked, although there is a checklist at the back of this book, so you can make sure you have all the elements you want to include covered. It is *your* wedding and can, therefore, be as simple or elaborate as *you* wish. One word of warning, however. If you do want to include several of these elements and time is short, you will probably need help from friends or parents. Don't hold back from asking them – you will find that people will be glad to help as long as they know what you want. Alternatively, you could contact a consultant to deal with the bookings, the preparation and planning, while you concentrate on each other.

The first thing you need to decide is what style of wedding you want, the location and a few alternative dates. If astrology is important to you then you may want to consult an astrologer to determine the most favourable day and time – be aware, though, that it might not turn out to be very convenient! This chapter will help you make your choices, get you thinking and start you on the journey towards creating your wedding. Then we will move onto the ceremony itself.

A SACRED, BEAUTIFUL
OR UNUSUAL SETTING

Your choice of location is probably the single most important thing you will need to decide. It will affect all your other plans and may influence what you wear, the style of your invitations, what you and your guests eat and drink and the entire atmosphere of your wedding. So decide first what tone you want to set: intimate, exotic, fun, religious, formal, theatrical or social.

If you do not already have a firm idea of location in mind, here are some options for you to consider:

COUNTRY

- Home.
- Anywhere else! The list is as long as there are countries and cities: a romantic city like Florence or Vienna, a tropical island, a boat on the Nile, or (for the entertainment-minded) the US. See Chapter 7 for more details.

VENUE

- *Your local register office or register office in another district.* Remember the change in the law allows you to look further afield.
- *Synagogue or other place of worship.* Clearly this will depend on your religious leanings and background.
- *Hotel.* Over 100 hotels across England and Wales have now been granted licences to hold civil weddings, notable examples being Horsted Place in Sussex, Land's End Hotel in Cornwall and Hintelsham Hall in Suffolk. Check current issues of wedding magazines for up-to-date listings, or look through Country House Hotel guides and phone direct. Many have produced their own wedding brochures detailing the packages they offer.
- *Stately home.* Cliveden is now licensed, as is Tatton Mansion in Cheshire and certain National Trust properties such as Clandon Park in Surrey. Contact the National Trust office in your local region for details.
- *Castle.* Personally, I think castles are utterly wonderful places to hold a wedding. Peckforton, Ripley and Caerphilly castles are available for bookings, with many

more queuing up to qualify.

- *Redundant church*. For religiously minded divorcees not permitted by their local vicar to marry in church, holding the ceremony in a redundant church can be an ideal solution. Contact the Church Commissioners (*see* Useful Addresses) for a list of redundant churches, each of which is managed by the secretary for each diocese. Since 1969 around 1,400 churches have lost their congregations and ministers, and many are lying empty.
- *Museum, club or livery hall*. There will be fantastic opportunities for unusual venues and 'theme' weddings once museums, art galleries and other slightly off-beat places start to be licensed. It's best to phone the venue in question to check availability. If they are not yet licensed and haven't considered it, it might be worth suggesting they apply – the licence may have come through by the time your wedding comes around!
- *Theme park, zoo, fun fair or holiday camp*. At the time of writing none have as yet been licensed (apart from London Zoo), but Butlins has applied. Great for fancy dress weddings!
- *Football club*. Aston Villa and Stoke City may now hold weddings, as can other sporting venues, such as Cheltenham Racecourse and Aldwark Manor Golf Club in Yorkshire. If you want it to be legal though, it has to be inside.
- *River boat or barge*. Approved premises need to be immovable, so only permanently moored barges may be licensed.
- *Cruise liner*. On board ship you will usually find an official who is authorized to conduct marriage services at sea.
- *Outside*. If you want to marry in a park, on the beach, beside a river bank, on a mountain, in a forest glade or under a gazebo in your own garden, sadly this is not yet legal in England, Ireland and Wales. You will need to hold a civil ceremony separately. If may be worth it, as open-air weddings are unusual and romantic. Add atmosphere

with candles or fairy lights, fill bowls with rose petals and scented water. Drape tables with lengths of material, hang muslin on walls, decorate with ivy, wheat, fruit and flowers; scatter herbs and spices on floors. If you are artistic you could even paint an evocative backdrop.

- *Up in the air or under water.* We're talking adventurous here: hot-air balloon, parachute, bungee or helicopter. Space is limited and it would need to be a post-civil ceremony 'blessing' of some kind. You will have to seek out an open-minded vicar or celebrant from one of the traditions described later in the book.

- *Hospital.* Nursing staff are usually happy to arrange bedside weddings, as long as the patient is not too ill. I did talk to one woman, Christine, who married her long-term partner Jim in hospital, while he was sadly dying of cancer.

- *Virtual reality.* Yes, it is now happening in cyberspace: at least one US company is pioneering virtual matrimony, which makes it possible to conduct your marriage anywhere without going anywhere, by means of electronic images transmitted through headsets. The bride and groom don identical 'vision immersion headsets', through which they are assailed by visions of hearts, doves and flowers while they are transported in a horse-drawn carriage to a castle in the sky. The computerized vision is simultaneously projected onto a video screen for the benefit of the rest of the wedding party. It is incredibly expensive, and I leave you to decide how meaningful it might be.

A CELEBRANT

A celebrant is the person who officiates at the wedding: for traditional weddings it would be a vicar, priest, rabbi and so on. Many couples feel it is appropriate to have their ceremony conducted by a 'wise elder', who will often say something about the couple, about marriage, about religious or moral guiding principles, if relevant, and about sharing a future together. This lends gravitas to the occasion and gives the wedding a wider meaning.

Depending on the type of wedding you choose, the choice of celebrant is very much up to you. If you want to marry in a particular church, the vicar usually comes as part of the package (although many are often prepared to share the service with another ordained preacher who is a friend of the couple). It would be a very open-minded vicar who would allow a rabbi or representative from another religious tradition to co-hold the ceremony, but, if you ask around, you may find one who is prepared to be flexible. A register office or other licensed building will have a registrar who will take you through the procedure in advance and conduct the ceremony. Other disciplines, such as the Humanists or Druids, will give you the names of official celebrants who will conduct weddings in your area – but you may also choose a friend or relative, or conduct the wedding yourselves. Some, such as Quaker weddings, do not require a celebrant at all, and the couple effectively marry themselves. See Part II for more detailed information on the different alternative wedding ceremonies and how to go about organizing them.

FORMAL INVITATIONS

If you were having a very traditional church wedding, you might feel very limited by convention as to what you should print on the invitation. This can lead to agonizing problems for some couples whose parents are divorced and have remarried, for couples who are marrying for the second time, or if the groom's parents are footing the bill. Even the size of type and the shape of the invitation itself follow a standard format.

This, from *Emily Post on Second Weddings* (Elizabeth L. Post, HarperPerennial, 1991), is advice on putting the invitation into the envelope:

> The invitation, folded edge first, is put in the inner envelope with the printed side toward the flap. The cards are inserted in front of it, with the reception card next to the invitation and any smaller cards in front of that. The inner envelope, unsealed, is placed in the outer envelope with the flap away from you.

I suggest you ignore this (even if you understand what it means!)

The joy of non-traditional weddings is that anything goes. Forget etiquette: from a phone call or a short, handwritten note to a printed card, the wording is up to you – just choose whatever you are most comfortable with. The following elements may or may not be included:

- your names (either just first names or names and surnames)
- venue for the ceremony
- venue for the post-ceremony celebration, if separate
- date and time
- address for RSVP
- any travel/accommodation instructions or suggestions
- appropriate dress
- a poem or quotation
- your parents' or guardians' names (if they are paying or hosting the wedding)
- your children's names

If you are artistic, why not design the invitations yourself and give the artwork to a local printer? Alternatively, there are companies who will design and print different stationery for you, with floral designs, gold, silver or medieval lettering, ribbons to match your colour scheme, or another motif which picks up the theme of your wedding (leaves and berries, for example, for an outdoor autumn wedding). Some do beautiful calligraphy and pressed flowers; some include sachets of confetti; others print invitations on balloons. Some will also design location maps for your guests. The invitations to a fancy dress wedding I once attended were illustrated with a child's drawing of the couple.

On the front of your invitation you could have a pencil sketch or photograph of your wedding location or a decoupage illustration. You could also print a few words:

And we shall become one
to share all the days
of our lives

If there is anything better than
to be loved, it is loving

Today is the first day
of our life together.

Today we begin sharing
our life . . .
. . . our love.

Two lives, two hearts
joined together in friendship
united together in love

We will share our tomorrows
and all that they hold.

Or choose a quote from an anthology on love, such as Eileen Campbell's *A Lively Flame* (HarperCollins, 1992).

Some couples prefer to give a special, formal touch to their invitations. For others, simple handwritten invitations chime in with the informal, natural style of their wedding. Again, it is entirely up to you, but it is a good idea to match the feel of the invitations with the feel of the wedding.

Alison Hollis and Geoff Wakefield
together with their children
request the honour of your presence at
their wedding
on
Friday 5th May
at 3 o'clock
in the garden of Abbotsbrook Hotel, Weybridge

Sarah and Katy
invite you to celebrate with us our
Ceremony of Love and Commitment
followed by lunch
on
Sunday 18th July
4 p.m.
at 67 Manor Road

If you are holding a party after your wedding – let's say you married abroad and none of your friends attended the wedding, or you are marrying for a second time – but don't want people to feel they need to bring gifts, simply send party invitations without mentioning your marriage. If guests then RSVP to a friend, the friend can explain your wishes.

No matter how informal your wedding, guests like to have service sheets or a ceremony outline. For alternative weddings, it can be helpful to be able to hand out a copy of the ceremony, or at the very least a guide to the proceedings. Many couples I spoke to said this was a good way of introducing their guests (most of whom had never been to an alternative wedding before) to the kind of wedding they had chosen. It also helps things run more smoothly if any audience participation is required.

SPECIAL CLOTHES FOR THE BRIDE, GROOM AND GUESTS

Traditionally, of course, the groom wears morning dress and the bride wears white. The white wedding dress was largely a product of the nineteenth century, a time when people were obsessed with virginity and purity. Silk, taffeta, chiffon, lace, satin ... most brides do want to wear something special, although rampant Mills & Boon is no longer quite the thing. Even traditional brides are now wearing understated, simple dresses. Remember, however, if you don't wear something that stands out, it might be difficult to pick yourself out in the photos – you definitely don't want to look like just another guest!

Muriel Gray, who married Hamish Barbour on a beach in the Hebrides, wore a daring (for the weather) off-the-shoulder dress made of tartan, while Hamish wore a kilt. 'It's the only day in your life you're entitled to go over the top,' she says. Advice endorsed by Paula Yates, whose beautiful, scarlet, duchess satin wedding dress and veil certainly looked dramatic for her (second) wedding to Bob Geldof. But beware the excesses of Brigitte Nielsen when she married Sylvester Stallone: her dress arrived in its own limousine and had to be escorted into the mansion where the wedding was held by three policemen. Or Masako Owada, who, on her wedding to Crown Prince Naruhito of Japan, had to wear court robes weighing 14 kilograms (30 pounds). And, of course, we all heard about *Baywatch* 'babe' Pamela Anderson and her white bikini wedding.

There are plenty of old folk sayings about The Dress: who sees it, the significance of the number of buttons, how soon before the wedding it should be finished, the fortunes of the seamstress who sews the dress ... most of which are redundant in this book, which seeks to leave tradition behind. I discovered, though, that while tradition may have been abandoned, superstition certainly hasn't. Even some of the most alternative brides still go for 'something old, something new, something borrowed, something blue', although fewer add 'a silver sixpence in your shoe', the forgotten last line of the ditty.

Here is an old poem about the colour or your wedding dress, which shows just how much times have changed:

> Married in white, you have chosen right
> Married in black, you will wish yourself back
> Married in red, you will wish yourself dead
> Married in green, ashamed to be seen
> Married in grey, you will go far away
> Married in blue, love ever true
> Married in pearl, you will live in a whirl
> Married in yellow, ashamed of your fellow
> Married in pink, of you he'll aye think.

It's your day, so make the most of your opportunity to do something wild and different. At a church wedding I attended once, the bride (who probably hadn't been in a church for years) turned up in a gorgeous bright pink dress and veil – the entire congregation gasped with delight.

Veils were originally used to protect the bride from the glances of jealous suitors. Today it's not essential, even in church weddings, but they can look rather glamorous. If you do decide to wear one you might want to choose an unusual colour and pile it up on top of your head, twist it round, or pin it up.

While it is true that anything goes at alternative weddings, choose something which suits your looks, your personality and the wedding. Here is a list of ideas for you to draw inspiration from:

- Dresses of silk, chiffon, lace or taffeta in any colour: cream, purple, red, green and blue were particularly popular with the non-traditional brides I spoke to. One woman dressed her bridesmaids in black, and some grooms chose to match their bride's dress, with patterned waistcoats, cravats or even white silk suits.

- Traditional dress from your or your partner's country or religious tradition, or to match the location or style of your wedding: Indian sari, Nehru suit, Chairman Mao jacket, oriental dress, baggy silk trousers, tie-die costume with rich headdresses.
- Authentic clothing worn at the time your chosen wedding originated: Elizabethan costume, Viking dress, Russian-style garments, plain seventeenth-century puritan clothing.
- Fancy dress: 20s, 50s or 60s – choose any decade this century – or go medieval, Victorian, or rock 'n' roll. Get your guests to dress up too, and have a masked ball afterwards.
- Evening dress: ball gown and black tie.
- Casual: T-shirts and jeans.
- Beachwear.

Get a dress-making friend to run something up for you, or try second-hand shops. You might even want to dye your mother's old wedding dress, or alter it to a more up-to-date style to suit you. If you are having a dress made, have the final fitting just before the wedding. And don't forget sexy underwear and garters, which I discovered were *de rigeur* with alternative brides!

Make sure your guests know what they are expected to wear, so they don't feel awkward in traditional hat and morning dress. Many alternative couples ask their guests to dress 'comfortably'. If you are going to be dancing, tramping through woods or sitting down at a picnic afterwards, plan your clothes appropriately. And remember, if your wedding is going to be outside, make sure you take umbrellas and warm wraps just in case. For foreign weddings, even if you are going to an exotic island, do check in an atlas for temperature and rainfall in the month of your wedding. Some couples get caught out!

Be careful not to let The Dress ruin the run-up to the wedding, as it can do for many a traditional bride. Yes, you want to look special, but every bride looks beautiful on her wedding day, no matter what she is wearing. As Nicola said, 'It truly would have meant the same to me even if I'd been wearing a cloth sack.'

A BEST MAN, BRIDESMAIDS OR SUPPORTERS

If you have chosen to have an alternative wedding, it is quite likely that you will be organizing it yourselves and may well need some extra support. The tradition for having supporters goes way back to pre-Christian times and appears in many weddings of different religions. In India, for example, brides go through a purification ritual before their wedding, where they are bathed and anointed with different oils by their women friends and relatives. In Czechoslovakia, a married couple, selected by the bride and groom, help organize the day and are responsible for leading the songs, cheering and the final placing of the 'apron of marriage' on the new wife as she departs with her husband.

Originally the best man was a friend of the bridegroom who helped him kidnap the bride. Although today you do not legally require a best man or bridesmaids, many couples do choose to enlist assistance. As well as helping in the run-up to the wedding, it gives a sense of support and 'groundedness' during the ceremony itself to know that you have your very closest friends on hand involved in your wedding and witnessing your vows.

Other options are to have a 'best person' each, perhaps a male for the bride and a female for the groom, who can take you to the wedding and give a reading or a speech. Or you could do as the Druids do and nominate five people to participate in the ceremony. Young children, favoured by traditional brides, can add to the fun and lend a family feel to the occasion, but they do need supervision and can detract from the solemnity of the ceremony by running amok. The most unusual choice of best man I have come across was millionaire advertising man Eric Forbes, who chose his dog Bobo as best man. Apparently the terrier turned up at Essex register office dressed in a £375 Versace suit with two rings in a pocket!

ARRIVAL AND HANDING OVER FROM ONE FAMILY TO ANOTHER

The couples I spoke to were divided on this point. Of course, in traditional church weddings, the bride is conducted down the aisle by her father and symbolically handed over to her husband-to-be. The groom may not turn round until she arrives at his side.

If you have been living together for some time, you may feel that as you are already established as a couple, it is more appropriate for you to arrive together as equal partners. In some Catholic countries, the bride and groom meet outside the church and walk in together, followed by the rest of the congregation. In Jewish weddings, the entire wedding party processes down the aisle led by the rabbi, with the bride bringing up the rear. If you want to do this, you may find an open-minded vicar who will agree. Or you could be escorted by a son, brother, mother or close friend, who could embrace you or kiss your hand as they hand it to the groom.

It is also often acceptable to alter the wording from 'who gives this woman to be married . . . ' to 'who presents this woman to be married', or 'who represents the families in blessing this marriage?' And don't feel you have to keep your back turned – you could copy the Jewish custom where the groom watches his bride walk towards him.

On the other hand, some couples like the ritual significance of arriving separately from two different lives, two different families, each giving their blessing on the couple who become one new unit. One way of having the best of both worlds might be to process to your wedding separately, followed by your families, and meet your partner outside the wedding, join hands and enter together.

A CIRCULAR FORMAT

No matter how alternative the ceremony, many women still want the feel of walking down an aisle to meet their future husband. If your father is involved, you may want to indulge his long-cherished wish to walk you down the aisle, even though you may be in a forest glade with seats arranged as if in pews. A circular format has ritual and spiritual significance, and certainly gives a wedding a different feel. It involves the guests more fully in the wedding and lends an intimate atmosphere. A circle will also allow you to be seen by everyone, but if you do have square seating, it is still possible to turn and face your guests during the ceremony, with the celebrant facing you or at one side. Alternatively, you and your partner can turn and face each other, rather than the celebrant, throughout the ceremony.

FLOWERS

No wedding, no matter how low-key, seems complete without flowers, which can add glory and charm to the simplest ceremony. Whether you carry a simple lily or have an extravagant display, flowers do lend beauty and freshness to wedding celebrations. Arranging them beforehand can be a fun activity for friends and family to share, especially if you have arranged the rest of the wedding yourself. You might want to consider including berries, herbs, fruit and wheatsheafs, for a natural, country feel. Tie your bouquet with raffia rather than ribbon: I always think a pretty, hand-tied bunch can be much nicer than a stiff, formal bouquet. If your budget is limited, you can achieve wonderful effects with small table arrangements in terracotta pots with candles.

The Victorians accorded special significance to flowers, which provided a useful code for lovers to pass each other coy messages. These are of limited relevance today, however, if you do want to know that a carnation means true love and a cornflower hope, there are plenty of books to guide you. My advice is to choose flowers for their colour, shape and price. For a striking display, go for exotic blooms like orchids and the orange and purple Bird of Paradise, or giant daisies in buttonholes and on the cake can be fun. One couple asked each guest to bring a sunflower, which made for a stunning, summery effect. Contact local hospitals and charities who may be delighted to have your flowers after the wedding.

MUSIC

Music is usually an integral part of any wedding ceremony: Shakespeare got it right when he suggested that it is the food of love. It adds mood and atmosphere and can echo the words or sense of the ceremony. It can also convey feelings that words alone cannot. Many couples choose reflective, quiet music before the ceremony, with an uplifting tune as the bride (and groom) arrive, romantic love songs during the wedding if there is a lull in the proceedings, followed by rousing, triumphant music when it is over. You can also use background music to accompany the spoken sections of your wedding.

If some of your guests are religious or used to traditional weddings, you might want to help them feel comfortable with the more familiar wedding tunes and hymns – but don't choose your music just to suit your guests. There is nothing to stop you choosing jazz, folk, pop, country, songs from films or musicals, love songs, harp, string quartet, swing, rock, reggae, steel band, sax and piano duo, trumpet fanfare, or a Scottish piper. The choice will depend on your taste and the setting and, some-times, the wishes of the celebrant – particularly if you are marrying in a church. But why limit yourself to music for your background sounds? For outdoor weddings you could play birdsong tapes or recordings of crashing waves, or simply hang chimes to sing in the wind.

Your favourite artists have probably recorded several love

songs, but here is a selection to get you going:

UPLIFTING OR ROUSING MUSIC

INSTRUMENTAL

'Trumpet Tune': Charpentier
Water Music: Handel
'Arrival of the Queen of Sheba': Handel
Trumpet Tune and Air in D: Purcell
'Bridal Chorus' (*Lohengrin*): Wagner
Music for the Royal Fireworks: Handel
Trumpet Voluntary: Jeremiah Clarke
March Triomphale: John Field
'Wedding March' (*A Midsummer Night's Dream*):
Mendelssohn
Processional (*The Sound of Music*): Richard Rodgers
'Pomp and Circumstance': Elgar

HYMNS

'Jerusalem'
'Now Thank We All Our God'
'A Safe Stronghold'
'Love Divine'
'Praise to the Holiest'
'Come Down, O Love Divine'
'Glorious Things of Thee Are Spoken'

SONGS

'Say You'll Be Mine': Christopher Cross
'Tell Me that You Love Me': Eric Clapton
'Space Age Love Song': Flock of Seagulls
'Stepping Out': Jo Jackson
'Perfect': Fairground Attraction

'Stand by Your Man': Tammy Wynette
'Never Gonna Give You Up': Rick Astley
'Love You': Syd Barrett
'Wouldn't It Be Nice': Beach Boys

QUIET OR ROMANTIC MUSIC

PIECES

'Jesu Joy of Man's Desiring': Bach
'Sheep May Safely Graze': Bach
Various choral preludes: Bach
Pathetique Sonata (slow mvt): Beethoven
Moonlight Sonata (slow mvt): Beethoven
Pastoral Symphony (*Messiah*): Handel
'Every Valley' (*Messiah*): Handel
Nimrod (*Enigma Variations*): Elgar
'Chanson de Matin/Nuit': Elgar
'Salut d'Amour': Elgar
Toccata in C: Pachabel
'Ave Maria': Bach/Gounod
Water Music: Handel
'Ave Venum Corpus': Mozart
Pavane: Ravel
Allegro from Sonata in F: Handel
Polonaise in A Major: Chopin
Gymnopedie: Erik Satie
'Summertime': Gershwin
New World Symphony (slow mvt): Dvorak
Serenade: Schubert
Selections from *Rosamunde*: Schubert
Cavatina (theme music from *The Deer Hunter*): Stanley Myers
'God Be in My Head': Walford Davies
Annie's Song: John Denver

SONGS

'My Beloved Spake': Patrick Hadley
'Sound the Trumpet': Purcell
'Laudate Dominum': Mozart
'Beati Quorum Via': C. V. Stamford
'A Love Song': traditional/words by Ben Jonson
'Ode to Joy': Beethoven/words by Schiller
'A Nightingale Sang in Berkeley Square': Manning Sherwin
'Close to You': The Carpenters
'I Could Have Danced All Night': *My Fair Lady*
'You're My Best Friend': Queen
'Amazing Grace': Julie Collins
'You'll Never Walk Alone': various
'Everything I Do I Do for You': Bryan Adams
'Riverdance': Bill Whelan
'Caracena': Bill Whelan
'Have I Told You Lately that I Love You': Van Morrison
'Wonderful World': Sam Cooke
'First Time Ever I Saw Your Face': Roberta Flack
'Stand By Me': Ben E. King
'Hopelessly Devoted to You': Olivia Newton John
'Part of Me; Part of You': Glen Frey
'Nights in White Satin': Moody Blues
'Perfect Day': Lou Reed
'I Want You': Bob Dylan
'Wonderful Tonight': Eric Clapton
'You Do Something to Me': Cole Porter
'Night and Day': Cole Porter
'My Favourite Things': Julie Andrews
'John Riley': The Byrds
'Blue Eyes': The International Submarine Band
'Bury Me Deep in Love': The Triffids
'Love Is All Around': The Troggs
'One Moment in Time': Whitney Houston
'A Long and Lasting Love': Glenn Medeiros

'The Best of Times': *La Cage aux Folles*
'Moongirl': Barclay James Harvest
'I Get a Kick out of You': Gary Shearston
'Loving and Free': Kiki Dee
'Nightingales': Prefab Sprout
'Broken Arrow': Robbie Robertson
'All of My Life': Diana Ross
'My Love': Paul McCartney

PSALMS

67 Let the peoples praise thee
130 Out of the deep
150 O praise God in his holiness

JOYFUL EXIT MUSIC

'All You Need Is Love': The Beatles
'Eight Days a Week': The Beatles
'You're the Top': Cole Porter
'True Love': Cole Porter
Polovtsian Dance (*Prince Igor*): Borodin
'I Was Glad': Parry
'Toccata': Widor
'Grand March' (Aida): Verdi

READINGS

This is your opportunity to add another dimension to your wedding through literary, secular or spiritual works. They can be joyful, contemplative, traditional or unusual. If read by friends or relatives, it is a chance to involve people who are important to you in the ceremony. The words spoken during a wedding are sacred, part of your own rite of passage. To enhance the vows you are making and the words of the officiant, add favourite poems or spiritual readings – even a love letter or words on a card your partner once sent you. If you can't think of anything immediately, visit your local library and scour love poetry collections, wedding anthologies or even dictionaries of quotations, which might jog your memory or lead you to a special piece. You could also make selections from different religious traditions. The *Talmud*, the *Koran*, the *Upanishads*, the *Bhagavad Gita* and many other sources too numerous to list here will all provide inspiration.

Here's a suggested list of starting points (unfortunately, there is not scope in a book of this size to print these wonderful readings and poems in full):

POEMS

'Two in the Campagna': Browning
'My true love hath my heart and I have his': Sir Philip Sidney
'Come live with me and be my love': Christopher Marlow
'One word is too often profaned': Shelley
'You are a part of me': Frank Yerby
'It is for the union of you and me': Rabindranath Tagore
'How do I love thee? Let me count the ways': Elizabeth Barrett Browning
'Shall I compare thee to a summer's day?': Shakespeare (Sonnet)
'If music be the food of love': Shakespeare (*Twelth Night*)
'Drink to me only with thine eyes': Ben Jonson
'She walks in beauty': Byron
'John Anderson my Jo': Robert Burns
'She walks in beauty': Edgar Allen Poe
'A dedication to my wife': T. S. Eliot
'Sudden Light': Christina Rossetti
'From pent-up, aching rivers': Walt Whitman
'Winter Love': Elizabeth Jennings

'September': Ted Hughes
'I wonder, by my troth, what thou and I did til we loved':
John Donne
'Dream of a common language': Adrienne Rich
'When you are old and grey': W. B. Yeats
'Love's Philosophy': Percy Bysshe Shelly
'Love': William Temple
'A Birthday': Christina Rossetti
'Now you will feel no rain': American Indian poem
'Your breast is enough': Pablo Neruda

BIBLICAL EXTRACTS

Love is patient and kind . . . 1 Corinthians 13:4–8a
Little children, let us not love in word and speech but in
deed and in truth . . . 1 John 3:18–24
Behold, let us love one another . . . 1 John 4:7–12
The Beatitudes . . . Matthew 5:2–4
This I command you, to love one another . . . John, 15:11–17
Extracts from the Song of Solomon –

PASSAGES FROM BOOKS

There are various books in which you may find passages to
quote, such as:

The Prophet: Kahlil Gibran
Return to Love: Marianne Williamson
In Tune with the Infinite: Ralph Waldo Trine
Healing the wounds: the promise of ecofeminism – Judith Plant
Soul Mates: Thomas Moore
Journey of the Heart: John Welwood
The Art of Loving: Erich Fromm
The Psychology of Romantic Love: Robert A. Johnson

VOWS

Whether you are writing your own or not, regard the planning of the ceremony, and particularly the vows, as an integral part of your marriage, not simply your wedding day.

What you are saying on your wedding day is that you love your partner. What you are promising is that you will love them tomorrow – and for ever. This is also a promise to grow together through the experiences life throws at you, through which you both are offering each other the chance to become the people you were meant to be. As Daphne Rose Kingma says in *Weddings from the Heart* (Conari Press, 1991):

> Marriage is an invitation to transcend the human condition. For in stepping beyond the self-focus of wanting only to have our own needs met, in schooling ourselves in the experience of putting another human being and his or her needs in a position of equal value to our own, we touch the web of transcendence, the presence of the divine.

The act of creating your own ceremony is an intimate and exposing one. Rather than allowing the traditional, familiar biblical words to wash over you and your guests, you are in effect stepping forward in a much more public forum to air the very personal nature of your own relationship. This makes non-traditional weddings highly emotionally charged events. As Christine said:

> I cried throughout, Mark was smiling but moved, most of the women in the audience and many of the men were in tears. Most people in the circle hugged or held on to each other as we made our vows. Once the ceremony was over, there was a spontaneous rush from everyone to hug and kiss us both.

There are likely to be people attending your ceremony for whom a non-religious wedding is new. If your words are sincere and reflect your own beliefs, you will find that everyone will respect your chosen style of wedding.

It is said that your vows will determine what your future life together will be like. I believe that what you say on the day will be what you get. And the more you think about and care about the vows, the better things will be. Many couples I spoke to wrote their own vows. Others adapted existing wording found in books. The basic format of wedding vows is as follows:

1) Declaration from both partners that they are willing to take the other in marriage.
2) Solemn promises from each partner to each other that they will love and care for each other, come what may.

You don't have to follow this format, but it does give a feel of being part of an ancient rite. In some Pagan weddings the couple take 15 minutes apart to compose their own vows there and then. They either declare them out loud or say them silently. Think about what you want to convey. Why have you chosen marriage rather than cohabitation? What does it mean to your relationship? What do you want to tell your guests about the meaning of marriage? What do you regard as important in a life relationship? Note down separately the key words and phrases which, for you, sum up your partnership and your hopes for the future. For example:

* how you met and how your relationship developed
* mutual love and support
* fidelity
* working through challenges together
* accepting each other's reality rather than adoring a mythical 'perfection'
* playing an active part in the community
* allowing each other the space to develop and grow
* children

If you are marrying for the second or third time, resist the temptation to refer to your first marriage as incomplete or inadequate. Look to the future and a fresh start.

NB: A registrar must be present and the legal wording (*see* page 88) must be included for your marriage to be legally recognized. If you want to say more than the standard vows, you will have to check with the registrar, design your own ceremony for after the civil occasion, or decide to forego a legal marriage.

In Part II you will find suggestions for different vows for different weddings.

EXCHANGE OF RINGS

Rings have been worn since the third millennium BC. Perhaps more significant than any other piece of jewellery, they have always represented an important emotion or new state: friendship, love or sorrow, or the promise of a marriage or a firm union. There are as many styles of ring as there are of wedding: simple bands or exotic rings encrusted with precious gems, plain or decorated with clasped hands, hearts or initials, or engraved with words of love or a motto.

An engagement ring containing your birthstone is said to bring you luck:

January: garnet – constancy, truth
February: amethyst – sincerity
March: aquamarine – courage
April: diamond – innocence and light
May: emerald – happiness, success in love
June: pearl – beauty
July: ruby – love, chastity
August: peridot – joy
September: sapphire – wisdom
October: opal – hope

November: topaz – fidelity
December: turquoise – success

Some may be superstitious about emeralds (bad luck), rubies (blood) and pearls (tears), and others may want to avoid the cliché of diamonds, as 75 per cent of all women go for an all-diamond engagement ring. There is no denying that diamonds are classic, beautiful and hard-wearing, and they do have a wider significance. They were once believed to have protective properties: the reflected light from the bright stones was thought to ward off evil spirits jealous of the couple's happiness. Their brightness is a symbol of purity, sincerity and fidelity and, one of the hardest substances in the world, they also signify durability of the marriage bond. They were even believed at one time to have a positive effect on fertility (especially if the stone actually touched the skin), and the Italians used to call the diamond the 'stone of reconciliation', convinced that it would miraculously smooth marital arguments.

To give and accept an engagement ring in Roman times (where the custom developed) was a legally binding transaction, signifying that a girl had been pledged to a man and was no longer available. You may believe that the mere act of wearing a wedding ring is not out of step with modern thought. Think again! Wedding rings have a rather primitive origin. Early man would capture a woman and encircle her wrists and ankles with chains to prevent her from escaping! Another ancient practice involved circling her body with a rope, which would both keep her safe from evil spirits and bind her to him. Even in seventeenth-century BC Egypt rings had a supernatural significance, linked by their never-ending band with eternal love. Ironically, the early Christian Church initially rejected wedding rings as relics of a Pagan time, but gradually adopted the practice.

In the past few years it has become common for the bride and groom both to exchange rings, although 20 per cent of men (presumably the more traditional ones) still do not sport wedding rings. In Germany, engagement rings become the wedding rings: they are simply moved from the left hand to the right. Jewish wedding rings originally served as a token of the groom's ability and pledge to look after his wife. They were decorated with a house, synagogue or temple, and were sometimes so ornate that they were not used as finger rings, but as a ring to hold the bride's bouquet. Nowadays they symbolize the sanctity of the marriage bond and (at least in the UK) are plain hoops made of gold or other metal, sometimes bearing the inscription *Mazel tov* (good luck).

The significance of wearing the ring on the third finger of the left hand is interesting. One rather quaint theory is the mistaken belief that a vein (the aptly but wrongly named 'vena amoris') from that finger leads directly to the heart; another is that the left hand represents submission and the right domination – clear messages there!

There is no reason why you need to choose a plain gold band as a wedding ring. You might like to consider the traditional Irish Claddagh ring which is used as a friendship ring, an engagement ring or a wedding ring. It was created in the sixteenth century by a love-lorn Galway jeweller, bereft of his beloved. The design for the ring came to him in a dream: a heart to symbolize love, surrounded by clasped hands for friendship and a crown to symbolize eternity.

Russian wedding rings are a combination of three linked rings, each of a different colour gold. They are seen by some as representing the Holy Trinity; by others as symbolizing the bride, groom and witness. Elizabethans wore a version of this called the Gimmal Ring. Other antique styles of ring include a French Love Knot, a Plaited Love Knot, a Buckle or a Clinging Ivy. Celtic Knots, Weaves or Celtic Scrolls are beautiful and often encrusted with diamonds or emeralds.

Victorian betrothal rings include the Pansy Ring in the shape of the flower (pansy from the French *penser*, to think), or the Forget-Me-Not in turquoise and diamonds. Rather in the same way as Victorians used flowers to send secret messages, they would also combine stones together whose initial letters spelt lovers' messages, such as DEAREST (diamond, emerald, amethyst, ruby, epidote, sapphire and turquoise). Gypsy-set rings were also popular in this period: wide, tapered wedding bands with stones set into the band. Look out for geometric Art Deco or Art Nouveau rings, which are both rare and interesting, or square-shaped wedding rings, which are comfortable. Some jewellers depart from the norm with triangular cut or fan-shaped stones.

There is still a sense of magic and superstition bound up with the wedding ring – a symbol of unity, signifying that wherever you go alone, you'll come back to each other again. But rather than a bald exchange of rings, why not place the rings inside large flower blooms and hand them to each other? Or even, rather than exchanging rings, exchange another significant token. Last year one couple in Alaska, both ardent members of the National Rifle Association, exchanged semi-automatic pistols instead of rings. (*The Times*, July 27 1994)

CHOOSING A RING

Here are some things to bear in mind when choosing your ring:

- Go to a reputable jeweller, and remember that you get what you pay for!
- An antique ring will hold its value, and old stones are often clearer and more subtle in colour than new ones. If it is more than 100 years old, however, it will be delicate and should be worn with care.
- Don't be afraid of auctions: prices of rings usually start at around £100 (although the top ranges are very high!) Phone Christie's, Sotherby's or Philips to find out when their next jewellery auctions are.
- Consider having one specially made, particularly if you have a friend who designs jewellery.
- Gold is alloyed with other metals to make it harder, and

the carat number refers to the amount of pure gold out of 24 parts of metal. 22-carat gold is almost pure and the most expensive, but as a result the softest, wearing down more quickly than the durable 18 carat. It is best to have an engagement ring made of the same gold as your wedding ring.

- The ring should be a perfect fit. If you can twist it round, it is too big. Clean it by brushing gently with a soft toothbrush in lukewarm water with crystal soda.
- Insure your ring.

A RECEIVING LINE

The prospect of a welcoming committee – composed of bride and groom, parents and grandparents – to greet all the guests one by one can be daunting (both for guests and hosts alike). Indeed, it can take up to two hours for large weddings, especially with a toastmaster calling out names! Don't feel bad about junking this idea completely, but remember that although you may be the hosts, you are not really in a position to introduce the guests to each other. If your parents are hosting the wedding, they may also like an opportunity to meet everyone. Even in traditional weddings there is no set time to have the line: as you come out of the ceremony, as you go into the reception, as you move into the marquee. Do make a conscious effort to get round and speak to people if you don't have a line. You invited them for a reason – to witness your vows and to enjoy your day with you. They will want to say a few words to you.

A POST-WEDDING MEAL

Depending on the time of day, space and funds available, it is generally regarded as essential to have some kind of party after the ceremony. Here are some ideas to choose from:

- Full English Breakfast
- kedgeree with Bloody Marys
- blueberry waffles with cream, fruit and coffee
- canapés
- vegetarian buffet
- full sit-down three-course meal
- fizz and cake
- fast-food (pizzas, burgers, hot-dogs)
- picnic
- barbecue
- oysters, caviar and champagne
- hot bread and cheese

If your wedding is small, you could ask guests to bring a dish each. If you are having a stand-up buffet, make sure there are a few chairs around for elderly guests or anyone who doesn't want to eat standing up.

For celebratory drinks, if you don't want to go to the expense of champagne, what about:

- hot punch
- an exotic pink cocktail: try mixing vodka, sparkling wine, orange juice and cranberry juice
- fruit cocktails and plenty of sparkling water
- Pimms
- wine: most off-licences will let you have cases on a sale or return basis and will lend glasses – allow at least half a bottle per head
- or there's always the pub

If you are doing the catering yourself, you will probably need to hire or borrow tables and chairs, cooking equipment, crockery, cutlery and an urn for boiling water. Neighbours may be able to lend freezer space.

Some couples have two receptions: one at the time of the wedding, another some days or weeks later – perhaps because many people or important members of the family could not attend the first. It could be a good opportunity to wear your dress again and eat wedding cake once more – but remember that it is a family celebration, not a re-enactment of the actual wedding.

CAKE

Cakes have made a relatively recent appearance on the wedding scene. Dry biscuits were ritually broken over the bride's head until the early sixteenth century, and as eggs, sugar, spices and currents became more readily available, the biscuits became small cakes – which were still crumbled over the bride's head in Elizabeth I's time. Inspired by French patisserie, marzipan and icing were later added, and with the seventeenth century came the custom for two cakes: sugary and light cake for the bride; rich and fruity for the groom. These two elements were eventually combined into the traditional iced fruit cake favoured by many traditional brides today. If you want a cake but feel that a tiered, formal, fruit cake, spiky with royal icing, would be over the top, as an alternative try a mountain of profiteroles shaped into a cone, topped with caramelized sugar. Alternatively, what about a huge pile of chocolate mini-rolls or a simple sponge or lemon cake? Many countries have special wedding cakes very different from our rich fruit cakes. The Norwegians, for example, cook a ring cake made from ground almonds. In Crete they make an elaborate, glazed, bread cake, adorned with birds and flowers. Bear in mind, though, that if you choose a non-fruit cake, it won't keep fresh for as long.

Feeding each other cake and drinking from the same goblet are old traditions which tend to be passed over these days. They are nice symbols of sharing, though, and you might also like to revive the custom of drinking a sour and sweet liquid (vinegar and orange juice, for example) from the same glasses, to represent constancy through good times and bad.

In Spain, silver charms are baked into the wedding cake. Each symbolizes a certain exciting future event, such as a baby, a new house, a marriage proposal or a tall dark stranger. The charms are attached to ribbons and all the single girls at the wedding are invited to pull them out before the bride and groom cut the cake.

SPEECHES

We've all been there – the ineffably dull round of tedious men holding forth about the groom's laddish escapades or the bride's exploits as a child. This is definitely a tradition which begs to be changed! You could dispense with speeches altogether, but if you have a long reception after your wedding you may find it quite good to have a focal point for the proceedings. It is also a chance for people other than the celebrant and the bride and groom to say something in public about the couple, and many couples like to have something said about them by an older friend or member of the family. It adds a formal 'acceptance' of the marriage and puts the couple in the context of their friends, family and former lives.

It is no longer unusual for the bride to make a speech – in a double act with her new husband – but consider also asking the groom's father, the bride's mother or a close female friend of the bride to do a 'best woman' speech. Another alternative would be to ask your guests to offer reminiscences and stories concerning the two of you, or to ask all present to bring a piece of advice for your future together. This might be a quotation, a poem or a song. At Christine and Mark's wedding, one guest performed a juggling act, as a metaphor for relationships, and another simply gave them badges with 'I am loved' on them.

SINGING AND DANCING

Nearly all cultures use singing and dancing as an expression of community and an integral part of celebrations and rites of passage. Many traditional brides opt for a disco, although this can often exclude the older guests. There is, in fact, a huge variety of music and dancing you can choose from, depending on the funds available. Go for a rollicking barn dance; lead your guests in traditional steps – Jewish, African, Thai, Scottish; or see the dawn in with a steel band. As well as music, why not include other entertainment (especially if you have younger guests), such as a bouncy castle or Punch and Judy show?

CONFETTI AND 'GOING AWAY'

The practice of throwing rice and confetti originated in Ancient Greece, when sweetmeats were scattered over the couple to bestow fertility and prosperity. At Malay weddings today, the couple feed each other throughout the ceremony with uncooked rice, and in Turkey guests pin money to the bride's dress. Paper confetti is difficult to clear up and, if wet, can stain clothes, while rice can feel like hailstones! A nicer and far more attractive alternative is a shower of delicate flower petals, so have a friend pass round handfuls of petals from a wicker basket as you leave. Remember, it can feel important for your guests to 'see you off' into your future together, so let them know in advance what time you plan to leave.

For a stylish departure, think about:

- pink Cadillac
- yellow American cab
- thirties-style Asquith Taxicab
- vintage soft tops
- motorbike
- bicycle made for two
- rickshaw
- hot-air balloon
- boat

- waterskis
- helicopter

A helicopter is good for country weddings (there is unlikely to be enough room for landing in town). Look for local air charter companies in your *Yellow Pages* and consult the back of wedding magazines to find companies offering other means of transport.

Fireworks will end the day with a bang, although you needn't leave them to the end: what about just after the ceremony (remember you will need relative darkness) or after cutting the cake? Normally the fireworks would be aerial, but you can choose a balanced display with some pretty ground effects. It is even possible to have a message lit up in fireworks, such as your initials around a heart shape: a lovely surprise for your new husband or wife, or to your guests as you leave. You will need quite a bit of space, about half the size of a football pitch, to prevent debris falling on your guests or their cars, who will need to be about 23 metres (75 feet) away.

You have various options for organizing the display:

1) Purchase a pack of fireworks and appoint a responsible friend to take charge of safety, site checking and firing.
2) Pay a professional firework company to provide the display from start to finish. This option would include insurance.
3) Alternatively, the company could put you in touch with a firer who, for a fee, would set up the display, fire it and clear up afterwards. You would need to be responsible for insurance, although if the display is held in the grounds of a hotel they may be covered by public liability insurance.

If you are in a built-up area or near an airport, it is advisable to notify the police, fire service and airport as a courtesy. If the display is near the sea then the coastguard should be informed.

WEDDING GIFTS

One of the most ingrained traditions is that of offering the couple a gift that will mark the occasion and remain with them for their married life. It is said that they also represent the breaking of family ties. Usually these gifts are of the long-lasting, household variety. However, if you are older and have an established home, have lived together for a while or are marrying for a second time, you may want something different. While it would be churlish to turn down an iron or kettle, think about including with the invitations wording such as: 'If you wish to give a gift, the bride and groom would appreciate . . .'. What you would appreciate is of course up to you, but here are some ideas for alternative wedding presents:

- donations to a charity or a park/woodland trust
- honeymoon vouchers (where a cheque could be a meal out or a boat trip – get a friend to organize)
- baby clothes
- gifts for your children
- plants or shrubs for your garden
- contributions to a car
- a honeymoon hamper (to include champagne, crystal glasses, chocolate truffles and mead – the legendary aphrodisiac)
- personalized champagne bottles
- food for the wedding banquet

SPECIAL TOUCHES

Unusual customs from other countries or religious traditions can be incorporated into any ceremony, whether or not you are marrying someone from another country or culture. With their roots deep in mythology, symbolism and folklore, the following traditions are archaic but charming and could provide another dimension to your own ceremony, as well as delighting your guests. Many couples like to retain a feeling of links with the past as well as creating a modern wedding relevant to their own lives. It is a good idea to make sure you explain what you are doing, perhaps in a note appended to the order of service. This will help avoid confusion, especially if audience participation is required!

A 'Smudging': a Native American ritual which involves burning incense or herbs at the beginning of the ceremony. Ask friends or children to pass a container with smouldering sweet-smelling herbs around the assembled company. This is a symbol of purification and preparation.

A Flower Girl: a young girl, three–five years old, who strews petals or potpourri in front of the bride and groom as they leave. Adapt this idea by having her scatter the petals in front of you as you process in.

A Wine Ceremony: this can be included in the marriage ceremony – not as a symbol of the blood of Christ, but as a symbol of life and the feminine. Both partners may drink from the cup.

A Ring of Stones: thought to originate from a Druidic tradition, make your vows inside a heart-shaped ring of stones.

Goblets of Mead: these can be exchanged instead of rings, if you want to keep the ring ceremony for another occasion.

A Loving Cup (or chalice): this is handed round for all the guests to drink from as a symbolic gesture of togetherness and hope for the future.

Floral 'Pooh Sticks': an Eastern European peasant tradition involving the newly wed couple casting circlets of flowers over a bridge to watch them drift downstream together.

Towncrying: a Romanian practice where the groom's friends ride through the village on horseback calling out news of the wedding taking place later that day.

Favours: usually bombonieres, gift boxes of sugared almonds or potpourri, given to every guest or a selected few. An alternative to Favours are Thank You Scrolls, which can be specially printed, tied with a ribbon and left on the place setting for each guest. Or why not hand out Angel (or affirmation) cards to your guests as they arrive.

A Loving Spoon: a Welsh tradition where the spoon, carved out of wood, is presented to the bride by a young girl in traditional Welsh dress. It symbolizes the ability of the new husband to live by the work of his own hands.

Jumping the Broom: an ancient Pagan tradition symbolizing the end of an old life and the beginning of a new. After your vows, simply clasp hands and jump over a broomstick or branch.

Throwing the Bouquet: don't feel you have to throw your bouquet if you have one – you might want to present it to a friend as a gift or have it specially preserved. In France a bride's bouquet is said to be medicinal: three leaves will cure a fever. If you have a circlet of flowers on your head, you could throw this instead like a Frisbee: whoever manages to keep a section will be guaranteed an early marriage! In Switzerland the wreath is set alight, and the brighter it burns, the more luck it brings. Greek brides sometimes wear evergreen headdresses, symbolizing long-lasting love.

A Book of Attendance: a relatively new practice is to provide a book for guests to sign – either just with their names, or with a comment, a piece of advice for married life, a poem or a quote. If you want something special written by each guest, ask them to come prepared. Alternatively, ask people to sign a copy of your vows, or a large sheet of art paper which you can frame later. Or you might want to leave space in your ceremony similar to that in traditional services for the signing of the Register. While your guests are listening to music, sign the book of attendance, which they will all sign after the ceremony is over.

A Board of Good Wishes: keep a pin board by the entrance to your wedding and encourage guests to pin their cards up.

Fertility Symbols: scatter rosemary along the aisle the night before your wedding, use sheaves of corn intertwined with flowers as a decoration, or get a local chimney sweep to come and kiss the bride.

Handfasting: a Pagan custom where both partners bind their hands together with twine or silk for the duration of the vows.

Proclamation: the celebrant asks the entire group of guests, or congregation, to pronounce you husband and wife.

Family Traditions: one couple took their first sips of champagne from an antique silver chalice which had been in the family for generations and was always used at weddings and christenings.

A POST-WEDDING TRIP

The word 'honeymoon' originates from the ancient northern European custom of drinking honeyed wine or mead as an aphrodisiac during the first month of marriage. It is still quite usual to take a holiday after your wedding, although some couples decide to have one *before* the wedding and others invite hordes of friends along. You can also combine weddings with honeymoons (*see* page 151). Quite apart from anything else, a honeymoon provides a wonderful opportunity to reflect on your wedding and your future lives together.

FOUR

FAMILIES
AND FRIENDS

FAMILIES

Even the trendiest of mothers may harbour secret fantasies of seeing their daughters float romantically through a traditional white wedding. Even the most radical of fathers may want to escort his 'little girl' down the aisle. Although most parents these days are so relieved their offspring are actually getting married that they are fairly relaxed about the kind of wedding they have chosen, don't underestimate the reaction you might get when you announce your plans for an alternative wedding.

This is what people said:

They weren't at all sure about the idea at first, but they have come round to the idea and liked the service we wrote for the celebration. I suspect my dad was upset at first about not giving me away.

Blessing following a beach wedding

Roy's family was impressed that he was getting married at all. Mine was a bit confused at first but then very supportive. Both our families supported us emotionally and got involved financially.

Gay ceremony

Both families were very supportive of the decision we'd taken and all really enjoyed the day. As Christians, I think my parents were pleased that we'd done it our own way, in comparison with people who do get married in a church without having any connection with it. One problem was that my parents saw it as their day as much as mine and wanted to invite a lot of their friends. We felt very strongly that we didn't want a huge event and didn't want it dominated by people Tim and I didn't know.

Non-denominational blessing

We both come from 'Christian' backgrounds. Our families knew we weren't rejecting this, just choosing what was right for us. They were delighted on the day and very excited by the project. Steve's mum said it was the best wedding she'd ever been to.

Open-air pacifist ceremony

My mother was very enthusiastic and excited – she helped us a lot. Peter's parents (who are Dutch) didn't really react. They probably thought it was a normal English wedding.

Open-air Humanist ceremony

Both sides were very supportive as neither follow any religion. They felt relaxed about their roles in the service, and were glad the bride's father didn't have to 'give her away'!

Humanist ceremony

I had only come out to my family a week before and felt it wasn't the moment to invite them to the wedding, although I shall invite them to the renewal ceremony one year later. Lee's parents are abroad and do not know she is a lesbian.

Lesbian Pagan ceremony

We came up against one set of angry parents, who could not understand our lesbian relationship. They arrived a little uncertain as to what to expect, but did eventually come with goodwill. Siblings, we found, were much more understanding.

Lesbian commitment ceremony

Everyone who could afford to come was delighted to combine the wedding with a holiday in the Seychelles. Unfortunately not all our immediate family or close friends could make it.

Tropical island wedding

My husband's family respected our decision, but apart from my mother and one cousin my family were strongly opposed. They boycotted the ceremony and kept phoning me to tell me that they thought I was selfish and unreasonable.

Viking ceremony

Our mothers would have liked a church wedding, but they were glad we were at least getting married.

Register office ceremony

It was difficult to gauge their reactions at the time. I think my prospective mother-in-law was relieved when we decided to get married, as we already had a child.

Civil ceremony

My family were all very pleased and agreed it was the best way to do it. We even had my grandfather's blessing, which is quite something as he is a vicar. They participated in the wedding by sending tapes, confetti and cards, and watched the video of *Honeymoon in Vegas* and drank champagne while we were getting married 5,000 miles away. My husband's family wasn't so keen and felt it wasn't very sensible – they probably felt left out, although we did invite them. We hoped they'd understand that we loved each other and wanted our own wedding. And anyway we were far enough away for it not to matter!

Las Vegas wedding

We didn't invite many family members, just four or five from each side, a reflection of the fact that our friends are much more our 'family' now. My husband's family was very supportive, despite the fact that his mother is an Anglican lay preacher. They were a little thrown that it was so alternative, but joined in enthusiastically and said afterwards – as everyone did – that it was a deeply moving experience.

Humanist ceremony

My family felt our wedding in Prague was in keeping with my personality, but were concerned that it all happened too quickly: we met, fell in love and decided to marry within a month. Jim's parents had reservations because they are orthodox Catholics and our marriage is not recognized by the Catholic Church. In the event, both families were delighted with the wedding, both location and format.

Civil ceremony in Prague Town Hall

With my family, staunch Catholics, religion reared its ugly head. Of the four invited, only two came. The two who did come had converted to the Baptist faith, and were supportive – but both said they felt we would have a more meaningful marriage if we invited God into it. I heard from one of these people that the rest of my family were concerned that I wasn't 'properly' married, and in fact two of my more elderly uncles, both priests, have now broken off contact with me because of the wedding ceremony.

Humanist ceremony

The love, support and acceptance was greater than either of us could have imagined. The ceremony has made us even more accepted by family and friends alike as a 'genuine' couple who are, and want to be, together. We are not just playing at a 'pretend' family.

Humanist gay 'affirmation' ceremony

Dave was told by his family, 'You can't do anything in a normal way, can you?' My father was concerned that our Mexican wedding might not be legal [it was], while my mother just worried about the whirlwind nature of the romance (we got engaged after only two weeks).

Wedding in a hotel room in Mexico City

To distil all the comments from those I interviewed into a single piece of advice is difficult. Many of those who had dug their heels in regretted it later; others did not. However, common sense suggests that you should decide how much you want to compromise on your chosen style of wedding *before* you announce it. If your mind is made up, leave no room for confusion and explain, gently but firmly, your reasons for your decision without blaming or getting defensive. If it is important to you to involve your parents, try to include some of their ideas.

FRIENDS

With very few personal axes to grind, you will find that friends are naturally much more happy to adapt to the wedding you have chosen. If your parents are confused or being difficult, you will need your friends all the more. You may even persuade one of them to talk to your parents. Low-budget weddings always tend to bring out the generosity in people, and unusual weddings generate excitement and interest. You'll probably find all your friends enter into the spirit of the occasion.

Here are some quotations from couples I interviewed:

My friends were very supportive. Several people said they wished they had done the same, or would do so. Some were rather confused by the whole thing!

Non-denominational blessing

All our friends were involved with the wedding – readings, speeches, ushers, helping with our outfits. Some were a little apprehensive about whether it would work, but everyone enjoyed it.

Ceremony of blessing and celebration in a garden

Our friends were very curious at first, very interested and totally supportive. Several friends with special talents helped out: one made the dress, another the rings, others made the food, took the photographs and lent their car.

Humanist ceremony at Milton Keynes Pagoda

My friends were great. They organized costumes and helped with the catering: a medieval banquet.

Viking ceremony

We were quite prepared to marry alone, but several friends insisted on coming to Las Vegas. Some felt a little upset that they couldn't come. In the end we had an international group of friends at the wedding, comprising Japanese, Americans, Koreans, Italians and English.

Las Vegas wedding

It was a very warm, emotional, uplifting and overwhelming occasion for ourselves and all involved. It was a very positive act for gay acceptance, to the degree that several gay friends stated afterwards that it had changed their perspective on life.

Humanist gay 'affirmation' ceremony

Before the ceremony our friends praised our congruence in having the wedding we wanted. After the event, they praised our sense of occasion, style and spirituality. We also arranged the wedding so that everyone had a task (driving the wedding car, reading, holding the bouquet) and there was no one who didn't join in enthusiastically.

Humanist ceremony

We had a team of 14 friends to help in the preparations and the ceremony itself. We invited all the guests to say something at the wedding, which felt very moving and special. Many people commented afterwards that they felt 'cocooned in love and happiness'.

Lesbian commitment ceremony

For us, the main problem was explaining the ritual significance of a Pagan ceremony as well as the parts they would all play in it. However, we found that, unlike our families, our close friends – both straight and gay – were very supportive.

Lesbian Pagan ceremony

The conclusion all these couples came to was: take the time to explain to your friends why you are having an alternative wedding and what it will involve. If you can, let them help with the preparations.

PART II

⑥

FIVE

THE CEREMONY

⑥

A marriage represents an ending (of an old life), a coming together (of the couple) and a beginning (of the new life). The ceremony in itself contains elements of all these. It is at once ritualistic and unique, solemn and joyful.

The following pages present a variety of ceremonies from different traditions. The only legally binding elements of the ceremony are the promises you make to each other and the pronouncement that you are married. You can pick and choose elements of each, but the basic format is:

Introduction (Convocation)
The celebrant welcomes the guests and asks them to remember the significance of marriage and to honour the vows you are making. Literally, he 'calls upon' those present to bear witness.

Opening Prayers (Invocation)
If you are having a religious wedding, this is where the Higher Power (God, your own Higher Selves, Mother Earth or whatever has meaning for you) is invoked to be present at the ceremony. It highlights the gravity of the ceremony and opens it up to wider meanings.

Address
Akin to a homily or a sermon, this is a message from the celebrant both to you as a couple and to your guests – usually concerning the commitment you are making

through marriage. You can either let the celebrant write it himself or design it together and include some personal notes. For a gay wedding, this is where you could introduce a political note.

Consecration

A spiritual moment in the ceremony, this is a time for prayers which will underline the sacredness of the promises you are about to make.

Declaration of Consent

The bride and groom speak out loud their intention to marry freely, willingly and without coercion.

Vows

The key moment of any wedding, when attention is focused on the couple binding themselves emotionally and legally to each other.

Blessing and Exchanging of Rings

A symbolic and spiritual act.

Pronouncement of Marriage

The climactic moment which marks the exact moment of marriage.

Final Benediction

A joyous end to the ceremony as the now married couple are sent out into the world.

NB: The above format omits the traditional Presentation of the Bride (i.e. 'Who giveth this woman to be married . . . ?'), which, if you decide to include it, comes after the Declaration of Consent and before the Vows. Readings usually come before the Address, but you could include readings and music throughout the ceremony, if you and the celebrant feel it is appropriate.

We will now look at a selection of various marriage ceremonies from different traditions: some ancient, others modern, some established, others tailor-made for a particular couple. They are printed in their entirety (without music and readings). You will be able to see how they fit, broadly speaking, into the above structure, although some do depart quite radically from it. I hope they will provide inspiration and direction for your own ceremony, and enable you to choose a wedding to suit *you*.

THE TRADITIONAL ANGLICAN CHURCH SERVICE

I have started with this as it is not difficult to understand why so many non-believing couples marry in a church. Beautiful surroundings, ritual, tradition, solemnity and a service that embodies ideals and aims which are timeless and relevant: faithfulness, domestic harmony, a mutual love and service, a stable environment for bringing up children and a sense of the couple's place in the wider community. Most Church of England ministers are content to conduct a wedding provided one of you lives in the parish (if not you will need a special licence) or you have both attended services for six months previously. A few will refuse non-Christian couples; some will expect to talk to you about the meaning of a Christian marriage; but most get on with their duties as master of ceremonies without making too much of a fuss.

The most traditional church service dates from 1662 and includes some wonderful, ancient, ritualistic words. However, if you have no sense of religion or do not believe in God, they may feel meaningless, despite their poetry and beauty. In 1928 the Church authorities made a concession to equality by offering the option to delete the word 'obey'. However, some people feel that couples who use the slightly more modern wording are still accepting a patriarchal ceremony in which a modestly veiled woman, dressed in virginal white, is handed over by her father to her husband.

It may seem strange to quote this service in a book on 'alternative' weddings, but many couples rush headlong into a traditional wedding without fully realizing the import of the ceremony. If the words and the true spiritual meaning of the vows you are making are important, and to help you decide whether or not the traditional church wedding is for you, I quote below the 1980 version of the Christian marriage service:

Minister We have come together in the presence of God, to witness the marriage of N and N, to ask his blessing on them, and to share in their joy. Our Lord Jesus Christ was himself a guest at a wedding in Cana of Galilee, and through his Spirit he is with us now.

The Scriptures teach us that marriage is a gift of God in creation and a means to his grace, a holy mystery in which man and woman become one flesh. It is God's purpose that, as husband and wife give themselves to each other in love throughout their lives, they shall be united in that love as Christ is united with his Church.

Marriage is given, that husband and wife may comfort and help each other, living faithfully together in need and in plenty, in sorrow and in joy. It is given, that with delight and tenderness they may know each other in love, and, through the joy of their bodily union, may strengthen the union of their hearts and lives. It is given, that they may have children and be blessed in caring for them and bringing them up in accordance with God's will, to his praise and glory.

In marriage, husband and wife belong to one another, and they begin a new life together in the community. It is a way of life that all should honour; and it must not be undertaken carelessly, lightly, or selfishly, but reverently, responsibly, and after serious thought.

This is the way of life, created and hallowed by God, that N and N are now to begin. They will each give their consent to the other; they will join hands and exchange solemn vows, and in token of this they will give and receive a ring.

Therefore, on this their wedding day we pray with

them, that, strengthened and guided by God, they may
fulfil his purpose for the whole of their earthly life together.

[to the congregation] But first I am required to ask
anyone present who knows a reason why these persons may not lawfully marry, to declare it now.

[to the couple] The vows you are about to take are to
be made in the name of God, who is judge of all and
who knows all the secrets of our hearts: therefore if
either of you knows a reason why you may not lawfully marry, you must declare it now.

[to the groom] N, will you take N to be your wife?
Will you love her, comfort her, honour and protect her,
and, forsaking all others, be faithful to her as long as
you both shall live?

Groom I will.

Minister [to the bride] N, will you take N to be your husband?
Will you love him, comfort him, honour and protect
him, and, forsaking all others, be faithful to him as
long as you both shall live?

Bride I will.

[The priest may receive the bride from the hands of
her father (it is not necessary in law). The bride and
bridegroom face each other, the groom taking her
right hand in his.]

Groom I, N, take you, N
to be my wife,
to have and to hold
from this day forward
for better, for worse
for richer, for poorer

81

in sickness and in health,
to love and to cherish, (or, to love, cherish, and worship)
till death us do part,
according to God's holy law;
and this is my solemn vow.

[the bride takes the groom's right hand in hers]

Bride   I, N, take you, N
to be my husband,
to have and to hold
from this day forward
for better, for worse
for richer, for poorer
in sickness and in health,
to love and to cherish, (or, to love, cherish, and obey)
till death us do part,
according to God's holy law;
and this is my solemn vow.

Minister   [receiving the rings] Heavenly Father, by your blessing, let this ring be to N and N a symbol of unending
love and faithfulness, to remind them of the vow and
covenant which they have made this day; through
Jesus Christ our Lord, Amen.

Groom   [placing the ring on the fourth finger of the bride's left
hand]
I give you this ring
as a sign of our marriage.
With my body I honour you,
all that I am I give to you,
and all that I have I share with you,
within the love of God,
Father, Son, and Holy Spirit.

Bride   [if only one ring is used]
I receive this ring
as a sign of our marriage.
With my body I honour you,
all that I am I give to you,
and all that I have I share with you,
within the love of God,
Father, Son, and Holy Spirit.

[or, the bride places a ring on the fourth finger of the groom's left hand]

I give you this ring
as a sign of our marriage.
With my body I honour you,
all that I am I give to you,
and all that I have I share with you,
within the love of God,
Father, Son, and Holy Spirit.

Minister In the presence of God, and before this congregation, N and N have given their consent and made their marriage vows to each other. They have declared their marriage by the joining of hands and by the giving and receiving of a ring. I therefore proclaim that they are husband and wife. [joining their right hands together] That which God has joined together, let not man divide.

[prayers]

QUAKER WEDDINGS

If you are religious but object to formal religious dogma and tradition, you might be interested in the Quakers, with their pacifist, radical and liberal roots.

Although they are part of the Christian tradition, Quakers use a variety of writings for their inspiration. Also known as the Religious Society of Friends, Quakers attend meetings which are quiet and simple – the only words uttered are by those who feel moved to do so. A Quaker meeting is based on silence, but it is a silence of waiting in expectancy. Through the silence the Friends aim to come nearer to each other and to God. There are no creeds, no prayers, no hymns, no priest and no pre-arranged service. The silence may be broken if someone present feels called to say something which will deepen and enrich the worship. In the quietness of a Quaker meeting those present can become aware of a deep and powerful spirit of love and truth which transcends their ordinary experience.

The Quakers believe that the ceremony of marriage should take the same simple, quiet form as the regular Quaker meetings. The bride and bridegroom, in the presence of both local Friends and those specially invited to the wedding, take one another as partners in a life-long commitment of faithfulness and love. Both husband and wife make the same promise, seeking God's help for its fulfilment. All who are present are asked to help by prayer and support, whether silent or spoken.

You do not have to be a member of the Religious Society of Friends in order to marry in a Quaker meeting, but you would be expected to attend meetings for a few months beforehand and may be required to be registered as 'attenders' (this would not necessarily mean you are committing yourself to become members).

The marriage takes place during a meeting for worship appointed for the purpose. The couple should go in as soon as they are ready, but it is helpful if the meeting is already settled. At the start of the meeting a Friend will explain briefly the procedure for a Quaker wedding. Early in the course of the meeting the bride and groom stand and, taking each other by the hand, make their solemn declaration of marriage. Importantly, there is no celebrant, with the responsibility placed in the hands of the couple, who marry themselves. Each in turn uses these words, which must be adhered to:

> Friends, I take this my friend (name) to be my husband/wife, through divine assistance (or with God's help), to be unto him/her a loving and faithful husband/wife, so long as we both on Earth shall live.

After this the Quaker marriage certificate is signed by the married couple and two or more witnesses. This certificate is read aloud by the local registering officer of the Society of Friends, either immediately after the declarations have been made or towards the close of the meeting.

Wedding rings play no formal part in Quaker marriages, but many couples like to give each other rings after they have made their declarations.

The meeting then continues as it began with a period of silence, during which anyone present may speak 'in ministry'. This can be a time when the man and woman concerned gain inspiration and help which continue to be sources of strength to them during their married life. It is also an opportunity for those who attend the meeting to ask God's blessing on the marriage and to commit themselves to supporting the couple in whatever way they can.

The meeting closes after the Elders have shaken hands. Everyone who has attended the marriage is invited to sign the Quaker marriage certificate. While they are doing this, the couple and their witnesses go with the registering officer to sign the civil marriage certificate.

If you are attracted by an exceptionally quiet, plain but very moving ceremony, the Quaker marriage may be ideal for you. There is nothing to stop you having a knees up afterwards!

UNITARIAN WEDDINGS

The Unitarian faith is less dogmatic than much of the Christian teachings. It grew up in the Reformation and is a form of Christianity that maintains that God exists in one person only, i.e. the doctrine of the Trinity is denied. Unitarians also reject the concepts of original sin and everlasting punishment.

In a wedding, the focus is primarily on the couple. A Unitarian minister will want to spend a great deal of time with you before the wedding, getting to know you and your partner, your values and beliefs. There is no set wedding 'package', although the ceremony does follow the familiar outline and requires you to utter the legally binding words (*see* page 00) if you want the wedding to be strictly legal. During your discussions with the minister you will be encouraged to talk about why you have decided to marry and what you want the wedding to convey: joy, commitment, love, planning for the future. You will be able to write your own vows (as long as you include the legal words), and there is no need to arrive separately or for the bride to be given away by her father.

It is a religious celebration, but some Unitarian ministers are willing to avoid specific mention of God and instead talk about the Spirit of Life. The minister will recommend some readings but may be ready to include your own selections. You will also find that they often take a more relaxed approach to the music you choose than Church of England vicars or Catholic priests.

There are about 150 Unitarian churches in England, 30 in Wales (of which half are Welsh-speaking) and only 4 in Scotland. Contact the Central Administration Office (*see* page 168) to find out where your nearest Unitarian church is.

JEWISH WEDDINGS

The Jewish ceremony includes two elements: the betrothal and the blessing. The groom places a plain ring (traditionally a family heirloom) on the bride's finger, and the bride signals her acceptance of the betrothal. The couple then stand under the canopy (the chuppah) while the Seven Benedictions are recited, which include prayers for the return of the Jewish race to Zion and the rebuilding of Jerusalem. During this they will drink wine from the same cup, after which it is crushed underfoot, in a symbolic representation of the destruction of Jerusalem and the Jewish hope for its restoration.

CATHOLIC WEDDINGS

Similar to the standard Church of England service in terms of content and sentiment, a Catholic wedding is usually longer, more ornate and includes Mass. The Register is signed during the wedding, and the registrar is present as well as the priest. Catholics regard marriage as indissoluble.

CIVIL WEDDINGS

Register offices have had a bad press. Municipal and rather dowdy in appearance, they may be efficiently administered, but do appear somewhat soulless. How many times have you driven past a drab town hall on a wet Saturday morning and seen groups of people queuing to be the 'next lot to be done'?

The simplest form of wedding a couple can choose, register office weddings must follow a standard form of words. It is difficult to express your own sentiments and values within this strict format, although the rules are relaxing and some register offices now allow couples to include their own readings and music.

The register office ceremony is as follows:

The ceremony begins with a short introduction by the Superintendent Registrar, who will ask each of you to repeat the following (legally prescribed) words:

> I do solemnly declare that I know not of any lawful impediment why I . . . may not be joined in matrimony to . . .

[At this stage a ring may be given to one of you or rings exchanged, although this is not legally required.]

> I call upon these persons here present to witness that I . . . do take thee . . . to be my lawful wedded husband/wife.

You may add any additional words at this stage, although this should have been discussed previously with the Superintendent Registrar. The Register is signed and you will then be presented with the marriage certificate.

If you hold your wedding in one of the buildings now licensed for that purpose, the ceremony follows the same lines as above.

SCOTLAND

Remember that in Scotland it is the celebrant – not the building – who matters. The legal wording is similar to that used in England and Wales.

A RELIGIOUS BLESSING

If you opt for a register office wedding, marry abroad and want a service when you return, or are marrying into another faith, a ceremony of blessing and celebration might be something you would choose. It could take place in a church, a synagogue, a garden or a hotel, and is essentially a more personal 'addition' to the official legal ceremony. The wording of the service would either conform to your religious leanings or could be entirely secular. The following ceremonies were sent to me by the couples themselves, were found in books, or are printed with the permission of various organizations. They are intended to be used not necessarily as a formal template for your own wedding, but as inspiration and guidance. Please note that readings and music have been omitted.

⑥

Katy and Peter (28, a cleric), who got married on a beach in Florida, arranged the following service of blessing in their local parish church for when they returned.

Welcome by Celebrant
We have gathered together to celebrate the marriage of Katy and Peter. Marriage is the promise of hope between two people who love each other, who trust that love, who honour one another as individuals in their togetherness, and who wish to share the future together.

It enables two separate people to share their desires, longings, dreams and memories, their joys and laughter, and to help each other through their uncertainties. It provides the encouragement to risk more and thus to gain more. In marriage, the husband and wife belong together, providing mutual support and a stability in which their children may grow.

We have come together to witness the promises of Peter and Katy in marriage; to share with them in their happiness and their hopes for the future.

Vows
In the presence of God and our family and friends, here I Katy/Peter declare my love for you Peter/Katy, and seek God's blessing on our relationship.

I will continue to love you, care for you and consider you before
   my own needs;

I will trust and be honest with you, in good times and in times of
   difficulty;

I will rejoice when you are happy and grieve when you suffer;

I will share your interests and hope for the future;

I will try to understand you even when I do not agree with you;

I will help you to be your true self and honour you as a dwelling
   place of God.

In all this I ask for God's help, now and in the days to come.

Exchange of Rings

This ring is a sign of all that I am and all that I have. Receive and
treasure it as a token and pledge of the love that I have for you.

Blessing
(All)

In marriage may you be a source of blessing to each other and to
   all,

and live together in holy love until your lives' end.

May God bless you and keep you.

May God make his face to shine upon you and be gracious to you.

May God lift up the light of his countenance upon you and give
   you peace.

Prayers
(Celebrant)

God the source of love

we pray for Katy and Peter.

Give them strength

to keep the vows they make

to be loyal and faithful to each other

and to support each other

that they may bear each other's burdens

and share each other's joys.

Help them to be honest and patient with each other

and to welcome both friends and strangers into their home.

Lord, hear us.

God of tenderness and strength
we pray now for all who are committed to each other in love.
May we be fulfilled through our love for each other.
Through our love may we know your love and so be renewed for
    your service in the world.

Lord, hear us.

God of peace
your love is generous
and reaches out to hold us all in your embrace.
Fill our hearts with tenderness
for those to whom we are linked today.
Give us sympathy with each other's trials;
and give us patience with each other's faults
that we may grow in the likeness of Jesus
and become more truly ourselves.

Lord, hear us

Amen

Blessing

The blessing of God
The eternal goodwill of God
The shalom of God
The wildness and the warmth of God
The laughter and the foolishness of God
Be among us and between us
Now and always.

Amen.

⑥

Alison and Tim (29, an airline marketing manager) also had a ceremony of celebration and blessing following a civil marriage. It was based on traditional lines, with vows, exchange of rings, homily and signing of a book: 'We wanted a feel of being part of an ancient rite of passage.' Alison's father, a non-stipendiary minister in the Church of England, presided over the ceremony, although he could not legally marry them.

Tim and Alison met together outside an open-sided marquee overlooking the Welsh hills. They made their entrance together, believing that to arrive separately – having been together for over seven years and lived together for three – would have been nonsensical. The readings were read by a friend and Alison's sister, and her mother read the address. The signing of the book was not simply for the couple and the family, but for all those present, to remind them who shared the day with them.

Consecration
(Minister)
Alison and Tim have decided to travel the rest of the way together. We are here to witness them commit themselves to one another and to this common journey.

Expression of Intent
Minister Alison, will you walk the rest of life's road with Tim? Are you willing to share everything, your whole life with her as she is with you? Are you prepared to make a total gift of yourself, body, heart and spirit to her, as he is to you?

Alison I am willing.

Minister Tim, will you walk the rest of life's road with Alison? Are you willing to share everything, your whole life with her as she is with you? Are you prepared to make

a total gift of yourself, body, heart and spirit to her, as
she is to you?

Tim I am willing.

Vows
Alison   Before these witnesses, this is my solemn promise:
/Tim

to love you and hold you always as my partner;
to stand beside you in good times and bad because
   my love is so great and your presence such a
   miracle;
to be tender with you and fierce with you;
to nourish you with my gentleness;
to uphold you with my strength;
to go with you through all the changings of age and
   infirmity;
whatever the sorrows or losses;
until we become true spirits in the end.

Blessing of Rings
Minister   Spirit of love and truth, bless these rings and let them
be to Alison and Tim, symbols of unending love and
faithfulness and of the promises they have made to
each other.

Exchange of Rings
Tim   I give you this ring
as a sign of our marriage.
With my body I honour you,
all that I am I give to you,
and all that I have I share with you.

Alison   I give you this ring
as a sign of our marriage.
With my body I honour you,

all that I am I give to you,
and all that I have I share with you.

Pronouncement

Minister In the presence of God and before these witnesses, Alison and Tim have given their consent and made their vows of union to each other. They have declared this by the joining of hands and by the giving and receiving of rings. We therefore rejoice in their union. Let us show our joy.

Signing of the Book

Blessing

Minister We pray that Alison and Tim will be blessed and guided in their journey, a journey which we hope will be a long and happy one. Above all, we pray that they will make the journey from selfishness to true love. Whether together, or single, this is a journey we all have to make. In a sense it is the real journey of life.

Miranda and Robert had a marriage blessing in Robert's grandmother's garden. They designed the ceremony themselves, drawing their inspiration from great religious traditions of the world.

Convocation
Welcome!

We are gathered here, as One, in the presence of God, our Divine Creator, to join in joyful, spiritual marriage Miranda and Robert, and to bear witness to the ever-evolving, transforming power of love.

To receive and to radiate Love, unconditionally, is our highest purpose and our most natural 'state of heart'. *Love is life's soul reason.*

Marriage is an embrace of souls. It is a whole-hearted dedication to surrender to love, to trust in love and to learn by love.

Miranda and Robert request on this day of celebration – and liberation – that each of us gathered here will, forevermore, give freely of our love, our loyalty and our support to their union.

Let us pray.

Invocation

Oh Divine Creator of all this Wonder, we pray that Your Love, Your Light and Your Joy may flow through us and around us at this time.

Both Miranda and Robert stand before You with heart and mind open and ready to receive Your Divine Inspiration, Clarity and Truth. We pray that You touch their hearts with Your presence.

May all of us who gather here as witnesses to the marriage of Miranda and Robert be blessed and uplifted. Please be with us, Dear Lord.

As we all say . . . Amen.

Prayer

God is Love, and those who live in Love live in God, and God lives in them.

Almighty God, we pray that you inspire us to become ever clearer emissaries of Thy Love, of Thy Light and of Thy Truth.

Guide us Lord to fill each and every day of our life with ever greater acts of kindness, acts of joy, acts of love.

May this world and all who dwell upon it be blessed this day and uplifted forevermore.

Consecration

Beloved Creator, Shine Your Mighty Light upon Miranda and Robert so that they may give wholly to one another in total joy.

Nourish their minds with Your Wisdom.

Enrich their hearts with Your Love.

Feed their soul with Your Peace.

Give them the courage and inspiration to honour joyfully the Vows of Marriage they make here today. And may the cherished promises they make to one another uplift in turn each one of us who are here to celebrate with them.

As we all say . . . Amen.

Expression of Intent
Marriage is a precious gift – a lifelong dedication to love. Marriage is a precious teaching – a daily challenge to love one another more fully and more freely.

With this understanding, do you Robert choose Miranda to be your beloved wife and to love him forevermore?

Robert I do.

With this understanding, do you Miranda choose Robert to be your beloved husband and to love him forevermore?

Miranda I do.

Exchange of Vows
Before the Presence of God, I Robert choose to be Your husband, Miranda.

Day by day, I promise,

to love you and to honour you,
to treasure you and to respect you,
to walk with you, side by side, in
joy and sorrow.

Day by day, I promise,

to hold you in my arms,
to grow with you in truth,
to laugh with you, to cry with you,

to BE with you
and to love you with all that I am and all that I
shall become.

This I promise you – from the depth of my heart, my mind and my
soul – for all our life together,

and if it is God's will
beyond this life and beyond the veils of time.

Before the Presence of God, I Miranda choose to be your wife,
Robert.

Day by day, I promise,

to love you and to honour you,
to treasure you and to respect you,
to walk with you, side by side, in
joy and sorrow.

Day by day, I promise,

to hold you in my arms,
to grow with you in truth,
to laugh with you, to cry with you,
to BE with you
and to love you with all that I am and all that I
shall become.

This I promise you – from the depth of my heart, my mind and my
soul – for all our life together,

and if it is God's will
beyond this life and beyond the veils of time.

Blessing of Rings

Beloved God, charge these rings with Your Love, Your Light and Your Joy.

These rings, with which you wed, are eternal symbols of individual and collective Oneness, Wholeness and Fullness of Life. Look to them, therefore, each day of your life together for your inspiration and common purpose.

Exchange of Rings

Beloved Miranda, I give you this ring in celebration of my love for you, and as a pledge to honour you and to grow with you for the whole of our life together.

Beloved Robert, I give you this ring in celebration of my love for you, and as a pledge to honour you and to grow with you for the whole of our life together.

Pronouncement of Marriage

As you, Miranda and Robert, have promised before God to give wholly and freely to one another, and to love each other according to your sacred vows and the exchanging of these rings, it is with great pleasure that I pronounce you – truly – husband and wife.

Those whom God has joined together may God generously bless forever. You may now kiss one another.

Benediction

INTERFAITH WEDDINGS

This is a difficult issue. Many religions will not accept marriage outside the faith, believing that it totally goes against the meaning of their religion and is therefore invalid. Religious families will often do everything they can to prevent it. As cultures and races intermingle, however, it is likely that more and more people will want to form relationships that cross these religious boundaries.

If you do go ahead with a mixed marriage, you will want to affirm and respect the traditions of each religion. It is a good idea to have two officiants, each representing their own side of the family, and to include readings and traditions from both religions. You will, of course, need to find officiants who can accept an interfaith marriage.

It is quite common these days to hear of Jewish/Christian weddings. Indeed, the foundations of the Christian wedding ceremony are firmly rooted in the far more ancient Jewish ceremony. For this reason, it is appropriate to include readings from the Old Testament, and readings from the New Testament which avoid the mention of Christ. There are some non-contentious hymns, such as 'Jerusalem', which are suitable, and a nice touch would be for the Jewish wedding prayer to be read (in Hebrew).

Nicola (26, a solicitor), who is Jewish, and Humphrey (26, a management consultant), a non-practising Church of England member, managed to make the standard register office ceremony moving and meaningful, inserting readings by Khalil Gibran, Shakespeare and an extract from The Song of Solomon. They followed the ceremony with champagne and cake for everyone who attended and then held a traditional Friday night supper for both families. The next morning Nicola took part in the synagogue service and on Saturday night they held a party for over 200 people, at which she wore a long white dress with flowers in her hair and he wore a black tie. Humphrey crushed a glass underfoot after Nicola's father's speech and the traditional blessing. They finished up, of course, with Jewish dancing.

BUDDHIST WEDDINGS

The Buddhist faith developed in India about 2,500 years ago. The constant search is for Truth, or Ultimate Reality, which is found within ourselves. Various yogic and meditational practices lead Buddhists towards this goal. Rebirth, rather than reincarnation, is central to the Buddhist doctrine, in which karma, or the law of cause and effect, is crucial. The five key precepts are to refrain from certain immoral actions, namely:

1) murder (which means that vegetarianism is preferred)
2) theft
3) irresponsible sexual relations
4) dishonesty
5) drink and drugs

Buddhism is becoming increasingly popular in the West, where consumerism and the fast pace of life has led to a growing sense of 'spiritual undernourishment', to borrow John Snelling's term (*Elements of Buddhism*, Element, 1990). Buddhism helps people find their own spiritual path, without having to follow a strict religion or strict techniques.

There are now many Buddhist groups in this country. If you are interested in learning more about it or becoming directly involved, see the Resources section at the back of the book. Buddhists advise newcomers to make a list of things they want to do in their life, and then to try living life according to Buddhist ideals for 100 days. At least one of you must be a Buddhist to hold a Buddhist marriage ceremony.

Although they do not have a wedding ceremony as such, there are ways of incorporating the Buddhist teachings and readings into a ceremony, such as the one chosen by John (34, a production electrician) and Janet (34, a sound engineer). They held a Buddhist ceremony after a civil wedding, conducted by a Buddhist Master with whom Janet had studied for some time. The format was as follows:

Entrance

The couple enter to the sound of chanting: *Nam Myoho Renge Kyo*, meaning 'I devote myself to Life'.

Ceremonial Gongyo

A shortened version of the ceremony performed every morning and evening by those who practise Nichiren Diashoin's Buddhism. It is essentially a ceremony of gratitude, and consists of the recitation of two chapters of the *Lotus Sutra*, followed by the chanting of the phrase '*Nam Myoho Renge Kyo*'.

San San Kudo: the Saki Ceremony (or the Ceremony of the Cups)

San San Kudo literally means 'three times three equals nine'. Saki is offered in a cup to the bride and groom, both of whom take three sips. This is repeated twice, each time with a larger cup, symbolizing the growing unity of husband and wife.

Vows of Determination and Commitment

This takes place in front of the gohonzon (scroll)

Exchange of Rings

Signing of the book

Address
(Robert Samuels, a leading Buddhist)

Marriage is without doubt the most important ceremony of life because, although it may seem paradoxical, upon the success of this partnership depends the ability of both husband and wife to give to this world their full creative value as individual human beings. Through their united resolve to create a wonderfully harmonious, yet essentially progressive, unit of society founded upon the rock of their deep respect for each other's lives, they draw out from each other the Three Poisons of anger, greed and stupidity, which might otherwise afflict their family life with misery for their lifetime. At the same time, through their victory in this struggle, they are able to send out waves of peace and friendship, not only to the community but the whole country and the whole world.

In the *Gosho* 'Letter to the Brothers', Nichiren Daishonin wrote:

> Women support others and thereby cause others to support them. When a husband is happy his wife will be fulfilled. If a husband is a thief, his wife will become one, too . . . If grass withers, orchids grieve; if pine trees flourish, oaks rejoice.

The relationship between husband and wife is the foundation of society because not only do they have it in their power to bring fresh new lives into this world, but also their home and family should be, in the words of our Buddhist teacher, 'an open fortress of faith' which is invincible to attack from the outside, yet is open to all who approach in friendship or with seeking minds; a firm base founded upon trust, from which the family can go forth daily into society, shining with the vital energy, wisdom and compassion which arises from the universal life-force flowing through their lives. Nichiren Daishonin explained it in the Gosho in this way:

> The hiyoku is a bird with one body and two heads. Both of its mouths nourish the same body. Hiboku are fish with only one eye each, so the male and female remain together for life. A husband and wife should be like them.

I hope you will think of these words of wisdom from time to time, especially when difficulties arise to test your fundamental respect for each other, because ultimately it is this respect, based on the dignity of life, that matters far more than the passion of love. I wish you much happiness and fulfilment throughout your lives together.

BAHA'I WEDDINGS

Baha'i is a religious faith founded in the late nineteenth century by a Persian mystic known as Bahá'u'lláh. His followers believe he was the latest in a series of divine manifestations that includes Buddha, Christ and Mohammed.

There are 6,000 Baha'is in this country. The key precepts of their faith are the unity of mankind and the unity of all recognized world religions. They believe in progressive revelation – that is, that Sikhism, Islam, Christianity and Judaism were all sent by God to mankind via a great teacher at various stages in our history. According to this belief, different social structures in the eras in which the religions developed led to the differences in the faiths. Baha'is strive for equality of the sexes, universal education for all and a world parliament.

A Baha'i wedding is very simple, pure and uplifting. You may hold it anywhere and it can include music, readings and vows of any kind. The structure is also up to you, although it is common to have readings from the sayings of Bahá'u'lláh.

The most distinctive characteristic of the Baha'i concept of marriage is the fundamental belief that marriage is based upon the submission of both partners to the will of God, and marriage is held to be an expression of divine purpose. Baha'is also believe that the aim of marriage is to procreate and that marriage itself provides a 'fortress for well-being'.

In the Baha'i community it is common to find marriages between people of different racial, linguistic, national and cultural heritages. You do not both have to be a Baha'i to have a Baha'i wedding, but you do need to do the following:

- Gain parental consent (unless you are estranged from your parents, in which case the Baha'i Governing Body in Haifa, Israel, would need to give permission).
- Have a legal civil ceremony within 24 hours of the Baha'i ceremony if you live in England or Wales. In Scotland, Baha'i weddings are recognized by the state and there are

five registered Baha'i marriage registrars.
- Have two witnesses and two representatives of the local Baha'i Assembly present at the wedding.
- Both of you say the following words during the ceremony: 'Verily, we all abide by the will of God'.

⑥

Nahid and Peter had a Baha'i wedding. Nahid (38, a haematologist) is a Baha'i and, although all Baha'i weddings are different, their ceremony provides a good example:

Opening Prayer
He is God! O peerless Lord! In Thine almighty wisdom Thou hast enjoined marriage upon the peoples, that the generations of men may succeed one another in this contingent world, and that ever, so long as the world shall last, they may busy themselves at the Threshold of Thy oneness with servitude and worship, with salutation, adoration and praise. 'I have not created spirits and men, but that they should worship me.' Wherefore, wed Thou in the heaven of Thy mercy these two birds of the nest of Thy love, and make them the means of attracting perpetual grace; that from the union of these two seas of love a wave of tenderness may surge and cast the pearls of pure and goodly issue on the shore of life. 'He hath let loose the two seas, that they meet each other: between them is a barrier which they overpass not. Which then of the bounties of your Lord will ye deny? From each He bringether up greater and lesser pearls.'

O Thou kind Lord! Make Thou this marriage to bring forth coral and pearls. Thou art verily the All-Powerful, the Most Great, the Ever-Forgiving. [Abdu'l-Baha]

Baha'i Marriage
Baha'i marriage is the commitment of the two parties one to the other, and their mutual attachment of mind and heart. Each must, however, exercise the utmost care to become thoroughly

acquainted with the character of the other, that the binding covenant between them may be a tie that will endure forever. Their purpose must be this: to become loving companions and comrades and at one with each other for time and eternity . . .

The true marriage of Baha'is is this, that husband and wife should be united both physically and spiritually, that they may ever improve the spiritual life of each other, and may enjoy everlasting unity throughout all the worlds of God. This is Baha'i marriage.

Marriage Tablet (read in Persian)

Vows
The Bride and Groom are invited each, in turn, to say:

We will all, verily, abide by the will of God.

Marriage Tablet
The bond that unites hearts most perfectly is loyalty. True lovers once united must show forth the utmost faithfulness to one another. You must dedicate your knowledge, your talents, your fortunes, your titles, your bodies and your spirits to God, to Bahá'u'lláh and to each other. Let your hearts be spacious, as spacious as the universe of God!

Allow no trace of jealousy to creep between you, for jealousy, like unto poison, vitiates the very essence of love. Let not the ephemeral incidents and accidents of this changeful life cause a rift between you. When differences present themselves, take counsel together in secret, lest others magnify a speck into a mountain. Harbour not in your hearts any grievance, but rather explain its nature to each other with such frankness and understanding that it will disappear, leaving no remembrance. Choose fellowship and amenity and turn away from jealousy and hypocrisy.

Your thoughts must be lofty, your ideals luminous, your minds spiritual, so that your soul may become a dawning-place for the Sun of Reality. Let your hearts be like unto two pure mirrors reflecting the stars of the heaven of love and beauty.

Together make mention of noble aspirations and heavenly concepts. Let there be no secrets one from another. Make your home a haven of rest and peace; be hospitable, and let the doors of your house be open to the faces of friends and strangers. Welcome every guest with radiant grace and let each feel that it is his own home.

No mortal can conceive the union and harmony which God has designed for man and wife. Nourish continually the tree of your union with love and affection, so that it will remain ever green and verdant throughout all seasons and bring forth luscious fruits for the healing of nations.

O beloved of God, may your home be a vision of the paradise of Abha, so that whosoever enters there may feel the essence of purity and harmony, and cry out from the heart: 'Here is the home of love! Here is the palace of love! Here is the nest of Love! Here is the garden of love!'

Be like two sweet-singing birds perched upon the highest branches of the tree of life, filling the air with songs of love and rapture.

Lay the foundation of your affection in the very centre of your spiritual being, at the very heart of your consciousness, and let it not be shaken by adverse winds.

And when God gives you sweet and lovely children, consecrate yourselves to their instruction and guidance, so that they may become imperishable flowers of the divine rose-garden, nightingales of the ideal paradise, servants of the world of humanity, and the fruit of the tree of your life.

Live in such harmony that others may take your lives for an example and may say one to another: 'Look how they live like two doves in one nest, in perfect love, affinity and union. It is as though from all eternity God had kneaded the very essence of their beings for the love of one another.'

Attain the ideal love that God has destined for you, so that you may become partakers of eternal life forthwith. Quaff deeply from the fountain of truth, and dwell all the days of life in a paradise of glory, gathering immortal flowers from the garden of divine mysteries.

Be to each other as heavenly lovers and divine beloved ones dwelling in a paradise of love. Build your nest on the leafy branches of the tree of love. Soar into the clear atmosphere of love. Sail upon the shoreless sea of love. Be firm and steadfast in the path of love. Bathe in the shining rays of the sun of love. Be firm and steadfast in the path of love. Perfume your nostrils with the fragrance from the flowers of love. Attune your ears to the soul-entrancing melodies of love. Let your aims be as generous as the banquets of love, and your words as a string of white pearls from the ocean of love. Drink deeply of the elixir of love, so that you may live continually in the reality of Divine Love. [Abdul'l-Baha]

Closing Prayer
Oh My Lord, O My Lord! These two bright orgs are wedded in Thy love, conjoined in servitude to Thy Holy Threshold, united in ministering to Thy Cause. Make Thou this marriage to be as threading lights of Thine abounding grace, O my Lord, the All-Merciful, and luminous rays of Thy bestowals, O Thou the Beneficent, the Ever-Giving, that there may branch out from this great tree boughs that will grow green and flourishing through the gifts that rain down from Thy clouds of grace.

Verily, Thou art the Generous. Verily, Thou art the Almighty. Verily, Thou art the Compassionate, the All-Merciful. [Abdu'l-Baha]

SPIRITUALIST WEDDINGS

Spiritualism is the belief that the dead manifest their presence to the living, usually through a medium or a clairvoyant. Spiritualists are a somewhat anarchic group. The Spiritualists' National Union is the main organization, although there are several other independent groups who may or may not be affiliated to a church. Some refer to God; others to the 'Great Spirit'.

A Spiritualist wedding would normally take the following form:

Welcome by the cantor (the secretary of the local association).
Homily on a relevant subject by a medium.
Trance – a medium goes into a trance and may give direct vocalization from the 'other side'.
Fair Witnessing – various people are asked to give a speech about the partners and the congregation is asked to witness. A medium witnesses for the dead.

Spiritualist weddings are conducted in those Spiritualist churches which have been registered both as a place of worship and a place for the solemnization of marriage. They are officiated either by a minister or a lay person, in the presence of the local registrar (if the minister or lay person is not authorized to marry people).

The following is the ancient version of the Wedding Service provided by the Spiritualists' National Union. Contact them for more information, including the modern version.

Prayer
Eternal Spirit of life and love, Father of all mankind, who, through the minds and experience of noble men and women in all ages, hast evolved the sacred bond of marriage to preserve the morality, and enhance the nobility, of the human race, shower upon us we pray Thee, the mighty power of Thy love, and bless us with the helpful companionship of Thy spirit messengers in this sacred hour.

May the strength and inspiration of the Spirit World be appreciably manifest in our midst, and the sincerity of the vows here made be recorded in the Higher Life.

[The couple plus friends and witnesses then say:]

We are come together in the sight of God and the Spirit World, and in the presence of this company, to join this man and this woman together in the sacred bond of marriage; to impress upon them the mystic significance of the marriage tie, and to seek the blessing of God and His messengers upon their union.

Marriage is an institution in the laws and necessities of our being, for the happiness and welfare of mankind. It has been made honourable by the faithful keeping of good men and good women in all ages. It involves the most tender and lasting ties that can unite human beings in this life.

As was said of old: 'For this cause shall a man leave his father and mother and cleave unto his wife, and they twain shall be one flesh.'

To be true, this outward ceremony must be the symbol of an inward and sacred union between two hearts and minds, which the church may bless and the state make legal, but which neither can create nor annul. To be happy there must be a consecration of each to the other, and of both to the noblest ends of life.

Minister If anyone can show just cause or impediment why these two may not be joined together in marriage, let him now declare it or else hereafter for ever hold his peace.

I require and charge you both, as in the sight of God and His messengers and remembering your responsibility to Him, that if either of you know of an impediment why you may not be lawfully joined together in marriage, ye do now confess it.

Couple I do solemnly declare that I know not of any lawful impediment why I ... may not be joined in matrimony to ...

Minister Who giveth this woman to be married to this man?

Will you take this woman/man for better, for worse, for richer, for poorer, to have and to hold, from this day forth as your lawful wedded wife/husband? Will you love her/him, honour her/him, and protect her/him, in sickness and in health, in prosperity and adversity, and leaving all other be faithful unto her/him throughout your earthly life?

Couple I will.

Minister What pledge do you offer that you will fulfil these vows?

Man This ring.

Minister From ancient times the symbol of the Golden Circle has been the sacred token of oneness, continuity and completeness; the outward signification of an eternal reality. Do you accept this ring in token of his troth?

Woman I do.

Minister You will place this ring upon the third finger of her left hand, and with your right hands joined, thus declare your marriage each to the other:

I call upon these persons here present, to witness that I . . . do take thee . . . to be my lawful wedded wife/husband.

For as much as this man and this woman have thus engaged and pledged themselves each to the other before God and these witnesses (both seen and unseen) I pronounce them henceforth man and wife. May Almighty God send down his richest blessing upon you both, that you may steadfastly perform and keep the vow and covenant now betwixt you made.

This is followed by an address, hymn, prayers and final benediction.

PAGAN WEDDINGS

Paganism is a general term for the nature-related spiritual traditions. Its origins go back many thousands of years, to a time when people worshipped the Earth Mother Goddess as the symbol of birth, death and regeneration. Pagans also worship the nature spirits: the sun, moon and stars. There are several different practices within Paganism, including Druidry, Wicca and Shamanism. Druidry is a highly evolved branch of Paganism, which today has several contemporary societies, such as the Order of the Bards, Druids and Ovates. This section includes examples of simple Pagan ceremonies and the more complex Druid weddings. You will notice that weddings in other sections of this book incorporate some Pagan elements.

In her book, *Rituals for Everyday Living* (Piatkus, 1994), Lorna St Aubyn offers a variety of Pagan rituals to mark various life stages or emotional events. Her rituals are designed to enable us to get in touch with the life force within ourselves and to sense an inter-connectedness with all life.

The marriage ritual in her book is an outward expression of the joining of the bride and bridegroom through their 'Higher Selves'. Ideally, it should take place outdoors, in order to access the energies of the living earth. If not, bring plants into the room.

Set a large flat stone in the centre of your space. Place two vases, each containing a flower, on the stone. These vases represent your two Higher Selves. If you are happy working with crystals, place one next to each flower, to represent the earth energy. Finally, put two candles on the stone, leaving space (to emphasize your individuality) between them and the vases.

Around the stone arrange a circle of candles, making sure

there is enough room for you and your two witnesses (if you are having them) inside the circle. Any musicians should remain outside the circle.

When you are ready to begin, both of you should light the candles, starting with one on the central stone, moving on through your half of the circle, and ending with the candle nearest the entrance. You then both enter this Sacred Space, standing one at each end of the stone. Witnesses enter the circle and stand behind and slightly to the side of you.

Make a silent commitment to each other, then each invoke your Higher Self to help manifest the love and joy created by this union. Then speak your vows, affirming that your love will not only be directed inwards towards each other but outwards into the world. Affirm, too, that you are each to remain separate individuals who must be complete in yourself in order to achieve a successful marriage. Lorna St Aubyn recommends reading Kahlil Gibran's poem *Love one another*.

The witnesses then leave the circle. You both blow out your own central candle and your own half of the circle. Leave the circle together, and dismantle the ritual site.

ⓑ

Sharon and James held a Pagan ceremony. Sharon, a Reiki Master, married James on Glastonbury Tor. They chose the site as the Tor is said to be the planet's heart chakra. Their ceremony was inspired by the myths and legends of the place, a sense of the oneness of the universe, and the teachings of Sai Baba, who teaches the religion of love.

The celebrant was a Pagan priest and the ceremony went as follows:

Address
Angels, magicians, wizards, and all good beings, join with us on this happy day and let this be a day of gladness, thanksgiving, possibility and great good fortune for all of us, but especially for

112

Sharon and James who are coming together to demonstrate the wonder of love through the celebration of their marriage.

Sharon and James, you are here because separately and for a long time, you have each chosen the path of self-knowledge. You have paid attention to who you are, what your life means and where you are going. But today, this day of your wedding, is the occasion of the shedding of your solitary journeys in favour of bonding yourself with one another, and your marriage, as well as being the estate of joining with another human being, is also the union of two people committed to the process of their own becoming.

Chalices

Sharon and James, I give you this healing water from the Chalice Well, so it may let love and compassion, trust and hope, freedom and joy enter your beings eternally.

Hand Joining

I join you in the name of Love.

Invocation

Marriage is a very special place, the sheltered environment in which we can endlessly explore ourselves in the presence of another and in which we can offer the possibility of the true reflection of another.

Sharon and James have now found one another, and they know in their souls how perfectly matched they are, and that they are choosing on this day of most special days to become for all time the accurate and beautiful reflection of each other's essence. We ask that the vision they have of one another be always informed by the spellbinding, radiant power that first brought them together, and we pray that as they move into the hallowed ground that is marriage they may always hold one another in the light of all light, the love of all love.

For them, out of the routine of ordinary life the extraordinary has happened. They have experienced the delicious stages of romance, to discover the love of substance and depth they are consecrating with marriage today. Romance is play, but true love is intention, and it is their intending to love for life that we are celebrating today. But today is also a celebration for the rest of us, for it is also a pleasure for us to see love in bloom, to participate in the wedding of two people so delightfully suited to one another. Therefore, Sharon and James, we thank you. You've brightened our day, and showed us that love can bloom, that marriage is a worthy enterprise and that happy, open-hearted people are overjoyed to undertake it.

Expression of Intent
Sharon and James, now that you have heard about the magic and the mysteries of marriage, the way it will continuously surprise you, the strength and wisdom it will everlastingly ask of you, do you choose still and happily and in our midst to make the promises of marriage?

> Do you, Sharon, want to marry James, to happily hold him above all and have him as your husband for life?

Sharon I do.

> Do you, James, want to marry Sharon, to happily hold her above all and have her as your wife for life?

James I do.

> Repeat after me please Sharon/James
>
> In the name of God and the universe
> I (Sharon) take you (James) to be my beloved
> husband/wife
> to stand with you in the bond of the love that binds us.
> To honour you, to change with you
> to open the windows of my heart

to behold the highest meanings of our being
to learn compassion with you
to be with you always.
I promise you this with my soul
from my heart, till death do us part.

And may all your days together be as the stars in the
sky, numerous and bright.

[hands untied]

Exchange of Rings
Sharon/James, repeat after me

I give you this ring as a sign and a measure of my love.
From this day forward your every breath
shall be surrounded by my love, today, tomorrow and always.

Benediction
God bless you, beautiful young ones. May the wings of angels
uphold you through all the life of your love, may you live forever in happiness with one another. May your hearts be full,
may your lips stay sweet. May your love grow strong, may you
live long and happily in one another's arms.

Pronouncement of Marriage
Sharon and James, now that you have heard the words about
love and marriage, now that you have shown us the example of
your love and celebrated your union with great joy and happiness, I ask the whole congregation to pronounce you husband
and wife. Please repeat after me, we pronounce you husband
and wife. You may now kiss.

DRUID WEDDINGS

Druids were magicians and poets, counsellors and healers, shamans and philosophers. In pre-Celtic times they built stone circles and worshipped Nature. Later the Celts blended the inspiring esoteric, mathematical and engineering skills of these megalithic peoples with their own flamboyant traditions of artistry and wisdom to create the Druidry described by the Greeks and the Romans. Although partly suppressed with the arrival of Christianity, Druidry continued to survive through the work of the Bardic schools and the folk traditions and customs of Ireland, Scotland, Wales, England and Brittany. Druid practice was revived in the eighteenth century and still continues today.

Druidry is based on a love for the natural world, and offers a powerful way of working with and understanding the Self and Nature – speaking to that level of our soul and our being which is in tune with the elements and the stars, the sun and the stones. Druids work to unite their earthly and spiritual selves, with care for the planet being an overriding concern.

The following Druid marriage ceremony held for Michael and Jane is taken from Phillip Carr-Gomm's book *The Druid Way* (Element, 1993).

⑥

[The participants form both a circle and a horseshoe, one inside the other. The Druid and Druidess who will supervise the rite enter. The Circle is cast by the Druid and blessed and consecrated by the Druidess.]

Druids Welcome.

All Welcome.

[The Gates are then opened by those at the Quarters.]

Druid   Let the Four Directions be honoured that power and radiance might enter our circle for the good of all beings.

North   With the blessing of the great bear of the starry heavens and the deep and fruitful earth, we call upon the powers of the North.

South   With the blessing of the great stag in the heat of the chase and the inner fire of the sun, we call upon the powers of the South.

West   With the blessing of the salmon of wisdom who dwells within the sacred waters of the pool, we call upon the powers of the West.

East   With the blessing of the hawk of dawn soaring in the clear pure air, we call upon the powers of the East.

Druidess   May the harmony of the circle be complete.

Druid   We stand upon this Holy Earth and in the Face of Heaven to witness the Sacred Rite of Marriage between Michael and Jane. Just as we come together as family and friends so we ask for the Greater Powers to be present here within our Circle. May this Sacred Union be filled with their Holy Presence.

[pause]

By the power vested in me I invoke the God of Love whose name is Aengus mac Og to be present in this Sacred Place. In his name is Love declared.

Druidess By the power vested in me I invoke the Goddess of the Bright Flame whose name is Brigid to be present in this Sacred Place. Her name is Peace declared.

Druid In the name of the Ancestors whose Traditions we honour,

Druidess In the name of those who gave us Life,

Druid and Druidess May we unite in Love.

Druidess The joining together of Man and Woman in the Sacred Rite of Marriage brings together great forces from which may flow the seeds of future generations to be nurtured within the womb of Time. Within every Masculine nature lies the Feminine, within every Feminine nature lies the Masculine. The interplay of Masculine and Feminine forces when flowing freely in a union based upon true Love finds many expressions. This union is truly Holy.

Druid Goddess to God,

Female Participant 1 God to Goddess,

Male Participant 1	Priestess to Priest,
Female Participant 2	Priest to Priestess,
Male Participant 2	Woman to Man,
Female Participant 3	Man to Woman,
Male Participant 3	Mother to Son,
Female Participant 4	Son to Mother,
Male Participant 4	Daughter to Father,
Female Participant 4	Father to Daughter,
Male Participant 5	Sister to Brother,
Druidess	Brother to Sister.
Druid	Who walks the Path of the Moon to stand before Heaven and declare her Sacred Vows?

[Jane steps forward]

Do you Jane come to this place of your own free will?

Jane   I do.

Druidess   Who walks the Path of the Sun to stand upon this Holy Earth and declare his Sacred Vows?

[Michael steps forward]

> Do you Michael come to this place of your own free will?

Michael   I do.

[Both walk the paths of the sun and moon (clockwise and anti-clockwise) around the circle, returning to the East.]

> Druid   Michael and Jane you have walked the Circles of the Sun and Moon, will you now walk together the Circle of Time, travelling through the Elements and the Seasons?

Jane and Michael   We will.

[The couple walk hand in hand to South.]

> South   Will your love survive the harsh fires of change?

Jane and Michael   It will.

> South   Then accept the Blessing of the Element of Fire in this the place of Summer. May your home be filled with warmth.

[The couple walk together to West.]

> West   Will your love survive the ebb and flow of feeling?

Jane and Michael   It will.

> West   Then accept the Blessing of the Element of Water in this place of Autumn. May

your life together be filled with love.

[The couple walk together to North.]

North   Will your love survive the times of still-ness and restriction?

Jane and Michael   It will.

North   Then accept the Blessing of the Element of Earth in this the place of Winter. May your union be strong and fruitful.

[The couple walk together to East.]

East   Will your love survive the clear light of Day?

Jane and Michael   It will.

East   Then accept the Blessing of the Element of Air in this the place of Spring. May your marriage be blessed by the Light of every new Dawn.

Druidess   All things in Nature are circular – night becomes day, day becomes night and night becomes day again. The moon waxes and wanes and waxes again. There is Spring, Summer, Autumn, Winter and then the Spring returns. These things are part of the Great Mysteries.

Michael and Jane, do you bring your symbols of these Great Mysteries of Life?

Jane and Michael   We do.

Druid   Then before all present repeat these words.

Jane   [facing Michael and handing him the ring] Accept in freedom this circle of gold as a token of my vows. With it I pledge my love, my strength and my friendship. I bring thee joy now and for ever. I vow upon this Holy Earth that through you I will honour all men.

Michael   [facing Jane and handing her the ring] Accept in freedom this circle of gold as a token of my vows. With it I pledge my love, my strength and my friendship. I bring thee joy now and for ever. I vow in the face of Heaven that through you I will honour all women.

Jane   In the name of Brighid I bring you the warmth of my heart. [Jane is handed a lighted taper by her mother or female participant.]

Michael   In the name of Aengus mac Og I bring you the light of my love.

[Michael is handed a lighted taper by his father or male participant. They both light a single candle together – this candle could be kept and relit at each anniversary.]

All   May the warmth and the light of your union be blessed.

Druid Do you swear upon the Sword of Justice to keep sacred your vows?

Jane and Michael We swear.

Druidess Then seal your promise with a kiss.

Druid Beneficent Spirits and Souls of our Ancestors, accept the union of your children. Help them, guide them, protect and bless their home and the children born of their union. May their life together reflect the harmony of all life in its perfect union. May they work together in times of ease and times of hardship, knowing that they are truly blessed. From this time forth you walk together along Life's Path; may your way be Blessed.

[Jane and Michael walk together sunwise around the circle to be greeted by each of the participants, then stand together west of centre.]

Druid It is the hour of recall. As the fire dies down let it be re-lit in your hearts. May your memories hold what the eye and ear have gained.

Druidess We thank the Powers of Love and Peace for their presence within this Sacred Place.

Let us offer the words that unite all Druids:

Grant, O God/dess, thy Protection
And in Protection, Strength
And in Strength, Understanding
And in Understanding, Knowledge
And in Knowledge, the Knowledge of
Justice
And in the Knowledge of Justice, the Love
of it
And in the Love of it, The Love of all
Existences
And in the Love of all Existences, the Love
of the God/dess and all Goodness.

Druid   Let the spirits of the Four Directions be
thanked for their blessings.

East   In the name of the hawk of dawn and of
the Element Air, we thank the powers
of the East.

West   In the name of the salmon of wisdom
and the Element of Water we thank the
powers of the West.

South   In the name of the great stag and of the
Element of Fire, we thank the powers of
the South.

North   In the name of the great bear of the
starry heavens and of the Element of
Earth, we thank the powers of the
North.

Druid   May the blessing of the Uncreated one,
of her Daughter/his Son the Created
Word and of the Spirit that is the

Inspirer be always with us. May the world be filled with Harmony and Light.

Druidess Let us now form the Three Circles of Existence.

[The married couple hold hands, forming the central circle. The participants in the outer circle and the horseshoe hold hands to form two further circles.]

All We swear by peace and love to stand
Heart to heart and hand in hand
Mark O Spirit and hear us now
Confirming this our Sacred Vow.

Druid This Sacred Rite of Marriage ends in peace, as in peace it began. Let us withdraw, holding peace and love in our hearts until we meet again.

[The Druid unwinds the circle and exits with the Druidess sunwise. Michael and Jane follow. Then the rest of the inner circle. Then the outer circle walk across the centre in pairs and out through the western gate.]

HUMANIST WEDDINGS

If you want a meaningful, non-religious ceremony to back up your civil service, a Humanist wedding is ideal.

Humanism is a view of life which has its roots in the teachings of ancient Greek and Chinese philosophy. It is based on the belief that human problems can be solved only by human beings and not by reliance on some supposed supernatural force. Since Humanists are agnostic or atheist, they believe in the scientific explanation for human existence, namely evolution. Their overriding concern is for human dignity and welfare, the ultimate aim being happiness and fulfilment. There is no 'book of rules' as such, but in common with many religions they support the golden rule: *do as you would be done by*. Humanists believe that religions and ideologies are not replacements for the need to take responsibility for our actions as human beings.

> Humanists look on marriage as a commitment that involves mutual love and respect. Each party has a responsibility for the welfare of the other, and to the success of the relationship. Where a couple have children the commitment involves a shared responsibility for their well-being and development ... The close and loving relationship of two human beings that is the central feature of marriage lies right at the heart of Humanism.
>
> *To Love and to Cherish (Jane Wynne Willson,*
> *British Humanist Association, 1988)*

Humanist weddings offer advantages to many people. They:

- are non-religious
- illuminate important values and beliefs while giving expression to two people's personalities
- accord equal status to men and women
- have a flexible approach to unconventional situations
- allow couples to choose their own words and readings, so that no two ceremonies are the same
- suit people who look beyond themselves and their family to express a wider concern for humanity
- can take place indoors or outdoors
- can include the couple's children
- are appropriate for gay couples
- provide a popular alternative to the traditional church/register office choice

Humanist weddings are not yet legal in this country, although other Commonwealth countries are more enlightened in this respect. Humanists are lobbying for a further change in the Marriage Act which would enable them to be official marriage registrars. It is difficult to find exact numbers of Humanist weddings being held in this country, as many people choose an uncle or friend to hold the ceremony rather than a representative of the Humanist Association. It is thought, though, that the numbers are increasing by 50 per cent each year. As Christine says, 'If you aren't totally convinced by a church wedding, go for a Humanist one. It has to be a better deal and one you will ultimately get more out of.'

> Neither of us is religious and we felt that a register office wedding was too formal and dull. We wanted to celebrate in a more personal way and, after reading the Humanist documents, we felt that it best expressed our reasons for marrying and our beliefs about society. We wanted a straightforward ceremony without any pomp or religion, so that we could feel relaxed and that the ceremony was relevant to *us*. We also wanted to marry in the place we met. If we hadn't discovered the Humanist ceremony we would simply have celebrated by having a party.
>
> *Diane (25, a teacher) and Simon (25, a journalist)*

> When we originally decided to marry, we rang the Registrar of Births, Marriages and Deaths (St Katherine's House) and established that it was theoretically possible to have a non-church ceremony. The registrar was helpful in fact, but a little off-putting, suggesting it wouldn't be 'proper'. I was amazed at the presupposition that only an Anglican (or at best Catholic) church wedding would be 'real'. Had we taken his word for it, we might not have proceeded further, and have settled for a register office wedding plus a wild party. Then I heard on the radio that the Humanist Association supported people wanting to hold non-religious rituals and rang them. From then on it was easy. They expounded at length on the phone about the joys of alternative

ceremonies, got us all fired up about different settings and ceremonies, and told us just how to go about it. Their booklet set out the basics and we took it from there.

Christine

PRACTICAL STEPS

1) *Find a celebrant.* The Humanist Association will give you a list of celebrants in your area, or you may have a friend who could perform the role for you. If you want to hold your ceremony in a church or chapel, you will need to find a vicar or chaplain who is prepared to conduct a non-religious ceremony. Unitarian ministers can often be more flexible (*see* page 86). Be careful in your choice of celebrant to guide you through the procedure of designing, arranging and holding your Humanist ceremony. Celebrants come from all walks of life and tend to have a flexible, non-preachy and open approach. They work on a voluntary basis. Christine and Mark adopted a business-like approach and interviewed three, considering each option and narrowing down their choice. They chose someone of their own age, outlook and values, who had experience of making a ritual work. Others prefer an older celebrant who will appear to be a 'wise figure' of some sort. The fee will vary according to the amount of time the celebrant spends with you, as well as the mileage involved.

2) *Compose your vows and choose the music and readings.* As there is no fixed format, you are at liberty to design the entire ceremony yourself. Your celebrant will be able to offer help and suggestions, and it is preferred if you include readings about human love and the family.

3) *Arrange details of time, place and format.* Check that the celebrant can be there (!) and decide on the format of the party, if you are having one. It is usually a good idea to have a rehearsal the day before, to ensure everything goes smoothly on the day.

4) *Give notice at your local register office if the marriage is to be legalized separately.* If you do this at least 22 days before the wedding, you will not need to get a licence and it will therefore be cheaper. Even if you do need a licence, there should be a gap of no less than a week in order for it to be legal.

THE HUMANIST CEREMONY

Humanist ceremonies do have form and structure and convey a sense of occasion. This, in brief, is the basic format:

1) *Introduction* by the celebrant, giving some background to the act of Humanist marriage and the couple themselves.
2) *Vows* ('aspirations' in Humanist terminology), which in order to be legal must include:
   I do solemnly declare that I know not of any lawful impediment why I (name, surname) may not be joined in matrimony to (name, surname); and
   I call upon these persons here present to witness that I (name, surname) do take thee, (name, surname) to be my lawful wedded husband/wife.
3) *Signing of the Register.*
4) *Congratulations and Address* by the celebrant.

The vows can be adapted and readings and poems added.

ⓖ

Christine and Mark held five meetings with their celebrant Simon before the wedding, and exchanged faxed versions of the ceremony as they developed it. On the day, he arrived with the final version neatly bound and presented it to them after the ceremony.

Christine and Mark felt that the whole event was a ceremony, with the party afterwards an integral part of the ritual.

Their ceremony took a circular format, the celebrant at one end flanked by Christine and her supporter, and on his other side Mark and his supporter. The full ceremony, not printed here, included several readings specially chosen to illuminate each vow. The ceremony commenced as follows:

Welcome
Good afternoon, my name is Simon Allen and I am here to help Christine and Mark at this pivotal moment in their lives. Whilst I am a stranger to you all, I hope that you will accept my good intentions towards your friends.

Opening of Ceremony
Christine and Mark have already attended a civil wedding for the benefit of the law. Now we are all part of their wedding ceremony for the benefit of them and, indeed, you all.

They wish to declare their commitment to one another in this personal and individual way. For them, marriage is not about how *other* people have arranged and conducted their marriages and lives. It is about *their* marriage and how they will conduct their lives.

You might be wondering why you are here and why we are here? If they are married in law, is that not enough? Not really, the law cannot encompass the warmth and affection, the shared experiences that have brought Christine and Mark together, or the dreams and sense of fun that they expect will keep them together.

So if they wanted to say something special to each other – why all of this? Well, the answer to that is *you*.

They could have stood in the kitchen any Thursday night they chose and say most of what they are going to say today – but you would not have been there.

So you might have thought that you were here because of them. In truth, they are here because of you. They want and *need* you to share this with them.

You are not here as an audience.

Your presence is an intimate part of this ceremony.

You are not present to hear recited words.

You are to listen to the taking of vows.

You are not here to watch a show.

You will witness their Rite of Passage.

The Vows

In most wedding ceremonies, the vows form a vital but only small part of the proceedings. Today, the vows – or should I say Marriage Contract – is the proceedings!

There are five vows contained in this contract. Each will be illustrated by a reading from one of us, and then affirmed by Christine and Mark .

The function of this contract is that Christine and Mark will take each other as Husband and Wife, in order to share their joys and sorrows in their day-to-day existence, and in order to pursue spiritual growth through each other's inspiration.

First Vow

The first vow is that: They will promise to love, honour and cherish each other for the rest of their lives, whatever the circumstances.

[Christine and Mark step forward and make the vow and then return to the circle.]

Second Vow

The second vow is that: They will promise to share their work, their home and their bed.

Third Vow

The third vow is that: They will promise to always be willing to negotiate.

The Fourth Vow

The fourth vow is that: They will promise to be honest with each other, in thought, word and deed.

The Fifth Vow

The fifth and final vow is that: They will promise neither to compromise with each other nor to be timid as they seek a glorious future together.

Confirmation from Witnesses

I call upon Melanie and Brian to confirm that they have duly witnessed the taking of these vows.

Melanie   I do confirm that I have duly witnessed these vows.

Brian   I do confirm that I have duly witnessed these vows.

[Melanie and Brian return to the circle.]

The Rings

Robert   By accepting your ring, I affirm my love for you and my lifelong commitment to be your husband.

Christine   By accepting your ring, I affirm my love for you and my lifelong commitment to be your wife.

Celebrant   In the presence of this assembly that has witnessed your words; I declare you husband and wife.

Closing Address by Celebrant

⑥

Darcy and Peter (26, a student, and 28, a management consultant) married outside a hotel overlooking the sea in St Ives, Cornwall. The Humanist ceremony was conducted in a mixture of English,

Dutch and Cornish (although I have omitted most of the Dutch translation here).

Introduction

Good afternoon. I would like to welcome you all to this lovely place to share in the celebration of Peter and Darcy's wedding.

Two years ago Darcy brought Peter to Cornwall for the first time. He then understood why she was so proud of her home country and the county where she spent the early years of her childhood. Their mutual love for Cornwall's tranquillity and natural beauty helped them to decide to get married here.

Although Darcy and Peter come from different countries, they have a deep respect for each other's culture and language and for this reason have chosen to say their pledges both in English and Dutch.

Peter and Darcy have come to love each other deeply and sincerely. They now wish to unite their lives and establish a home together. In this ceremony they make a public commitment of this, as they dedicate themselves to the happiness and well-being of each other. Marriage is a sharing of experience and an adventure in the most intimate of human relationships. It is a joyous union of a man and a woman whose comradeship and mutual understanding has flowered into love.

Darcy and Peter have chosen to be married in this Humanist wedding ceremony. Humanism sees a human being as an active and inseparable unity of body and personality. Reason is the guide, but a reason that is part of the emotions and strivings of the whole person; so that emotion and intellect together can provide a firm foundation for married love. Peter and Darcy hold in common the interests and ideals of a Humanist world. Living together in this way, they will deepen their love for each other.

It is a Humanist belief that there should be equality between men and women in every relevant way, and that it is especially important for this principle to be recognized in the marriage relationship. Marriage must be a co-operative venture. It is a relationship based on love, respect and a determination on the part of both wife and husband to adjust to each other's temperaments and moods – in health or sickness, joy or sadness, ease or hardship. The family has continued to show great hardihood as an institution and thrives throughout the world. In an age when many traditional values have crumbled, it becomes all the more important to recognize the significance of devoted and affectionate family life.

Peter, will you have Maria Darcy Jane to be your wedded wife, to share your life with her, and do you pledge that you will love, honour and care for her in all the varying circumstances of your lives together?

Peter   *Ja, ik beloof dat.*

Celebrant Darcy, will you have Peter to be your wedded husband, to share your life with him, and do you pledge that you will love, honour and care for him in tenderness and affection through all the varying experiences of your lives together?

Darcy   I will.
Peter, I acknowledge my love and respect for you and invite you to share my life as I hope to share yours. I promise to recognize you as an equal individual at all times, and to be conscious of your development as well as my own. I shall seek through kindness and understanding to achieve with you the life we have envisioned together. In token of my love and devotion, I place this ring on your finger.

Peter   Darcy, I acknowledge my love and respect for you and invite you to share my life as I hope to share yours. I promise to recognize you as an equal individual at all times, and to be conscious of your development as well as my own. I shall seek through kindness and understanding to achieve with you the life we have envisioned together. In token of my love and devotion, I place this ring on your finger.

Celebrant I now pronounce you husband and wife.
Hierbij verklaar ik jullie man en vrouw
My a vynn avowa lemmyn aga box gour ha gwrek.

As part of this celebration I will now read these lines from an American Indian ceremony.

Now you will each feel no rain, for each will be shelter for the other.
Now you will feel no cold, for each of you will be warmth to the other.
Now there is no loneliness.
Now you are two persons, but there is only one life before you.
Go now to your dwelling to enter into the days of your life together.
And may your days be good and long upon the earth.

Sowena Re'gas bo!

We rejoice as Darcy and Peter have proclaimed their love to the world and offer all our congratulations to them. You are all asked to witness this celebration by signing in the book provided.

Keslowena dhe Darcy ha Peter.

VIKING WEDDINGS

The basic format of a Viking wedding is very simple: the groom approaches the woman's father or guardian and makes an offer for her. The groom's family must agree to pay a 'bride price' and the bride's family must give a dowry (the more the better, as family honour is at stake). The money is to be invested for use by the couple, and is to ensure financial security for her and her children in the case of a divorce (provided her husband is at fault). Terms of the marriage are negotiated and a date is fixed for the wedding.

Guests sit arranged in three groups. At one end of the room are the women from both families. They are flanked on their left by the men from the groom's family, and on their right by the bride's male relatives. The ceremony consists of the handing over of the bride price and dowry in front of three witnesses, and then a banquet is held, with musical entertainment between each course. Clearly, this is only legal if you go through the civil ceremony first.

Nicola and Alasdair's interest in Viking society grew out of their involvement with archaeology and re-enactment groups, which attempt to recreate the way people lived in the tenth and eleventh centuries. They researched Viking weddings using historical and literary sources, and by consulting a friend who acted as 'law speaker' in their group. At their register office ceremony on the morning before the Viking ceremony, the best man wore full plate armour from the sixteenth century, Nicola a black cloak and veil, and Alasdair a black swede jacket with puff sleeves and red silk lining. Their wedding rings were engraved with Viking runes.

PACIFIST WEDDINGS

Pacifism is a philosophy based on opposition to war and other violence. Although it gained its label in the twentieth century, it is much older than Christianity, and infuses the teachings of many Eastern religions. Pacifists either work actively towards achieving a society in which war cannot happen, or simply lead a life free of aggression in any form.

(6)

Maria and Stephen held an open-air pacifist ceremony in a forest. They conducted it themselves, facing their guests. As an introduction, Steve thanked everyone for coming. After the readings they explained their values of pacifism, non-aggression and vegetarianism. After more readings and songs, they exchanged rings:

Maria   Stephen, I will feed you. [feeds Stephen a piece of basti, an Indian sweet]
Stephen, I will clothe you. [places ring on his finger]
Stephen, I will comfort you [hugs him] and I will always love you Stephen.

Stephen   Maria, I will feed you. [feeds Maria a piece of basti]
Maria, I will clothe you. [places ring on her finger]
Maria, I will comfort you [hugs her] and I will always love you Maria.

[At this, the couple jumped over a branch, a Wiccan tradition, representing the transition from the previous family to a new one.]

SIX

GAY AND LESBIAN CEREMONIES

❻

D
enmark was the first country in the world to grant homosexuals similar rights in marriage to those of heterosexuals when it introduced its 'partnership law' in 1989. These benefits, however, can only be achieved through a civil ceremony and not a religious ceremony.

In Britain any similar change in the law is unlikely, especially while the attitude of the Church of England remains firmly against homosexuality (although you may find a Unitarian minister who is more open-minded and prepared to conduct a ceremony). However, lesbians and gays can still have a ceremony which, although not legally binding, provides the opportunity to make a public declaration of their love and commitment to each other.

Despite the inflexible attitude adopted by many Christians today, there is a Christian movement, established 20 years ago, which believes sexual orientation is an 'innocent accident' and should be understood; not condemned. The aims of this organization are, amongst others, to encourage friendship and support among lesbian and gay Christians, and to help the whole Church re-examine its understanding of human sexuality. For a small fee, they will put you in touch with a minister or priest with whom you can discuss the possibility of a blessing on your relationship. They also provide a certificate to commemorate the occasion.

The Humanists have designed a ceremony specifically with

lesbians and gays in mind. The basic tenets of Humanist ideology are set out on page 125. Of particular relevance to lesbian and gays, however, is the Humanist belief in the Open Society, in which all are free to live their lives without interference, provided they do no harm to others. As Professor Sir Herman Bondi, President of the British Humanist Association, declared in 1988, 'Sexuality is an enormously important characteristic of human beings, which finds many different kinds of expression. To say that we know that only one is "right" shows a degree of intolerance which I find most objectionable.' In 1990, a motion was unanimously carried at the conference of the BHA, to the effect that:

> This AGM reaffirms its support for the rights of lesbians and gays. It deplores the hostility directed against them, particularly from religious sources and the tabloid press. It calls upon the Humanist movement and individuals to do everything possible to counter such hostility and to promote lesbian and gay rights as human rights.

Founded in 1979, the Gay and Lesbian Humanist Association (GALHA) is active in promoting equal rights for lesbians and gays. They have devised an 'affirmation' ceremony for lesbian and gay couples who wish to make a public statement of their love and commitment to each other. It can take place either at the couple's home, a friend's home or a public place where a room can be hired for the occasion. GALHA can put you in touch with a celebrant who will discuss the ceremony with you. Alternatively, you can get a friend to officiate.

This is the basic format of the ceremony recommended by GALHA.

The Entry
In most cases those present as witnesses will be assembled in the room prior to the couple's arrival. The officiant can either stand near the entrance to meet the couple, or stand at a suitable

place in the room and allow the couple to approach, accompanied by music.

The Opening

Once the music has stopped, the officiant makes a short opening statement welcoming those present and explaining that they are officiating on behalf of the Gay and Lesbian Humanist Association, which provides this type of ceremony as a service to the lesbian and gay community, and that the couple (giving their names) have invited their friends and/or relatives to witness their commitment to one another.

The Ceremony

The officiant begins the ceremony by saying:

We have come together to witness the joining together of two lives. In the words of Shakespeare's sonnet:

> Let me not to the marriage of true minds
> Admit impediment. Love is not love
> Which alters when it alteration finds,
> Or bends with the remover to remove:
> O, No! It is an ever-fixed mark,
> That looks on tempests and is never shaken,
> It is the star to every wandering barque
> Whose worth's unknown, although its height be taken
> Love's not Time's fool, though rosy lips and cheeks
> Within his bending sickle's compass come;
> Love alters not with the brief hours and weeks,
> But bears it out even to the edge of doom.
> If this be effort, and upon me proved,
> I never writ, nor no man ever loved.

(NB: The couple can replace this with a favourite poem if they prefer.)

(Name) and (Name) have come here in affection and honour to

say before us that they will henceforth share their home, and combine in mutual living and responsibility.

Love is the wish of the whole self to unite with another to the end of personal completeness. Touched by this love, nature yields tenderness, togetherness, simplicity, honesty and delight.

When two people openly and sincerely declare their affection for each other, they are affirming the precious truth that love is the foundation of all life – between two people, between friends and between all humanity.

I now ask you both [addressing the couple] to speak in truth to one another and to repeat in the spirit of faithful engagement these words of solemn declaration that bind you together. Will you (name) say after me:

> I want it to be known to all those present
> that I (name)
> take (name) to be my lover
> and promise to cherish,
> love and comfort him (or her)
> for all my life.
> I offer you this ring
> as a symbol of our love.

Will you (name) say after me:

> I want it to be known to all those present
> that I (name)
> take (name) to be my lover
> and promise to cherish,
> love and comfort him (or her)
> for all my life.
> I offer you this ring
> as a symbol of our love.

Now together, repeat after me these words:

> We have openly declared our love for each other
> and do pledge ourselves
> to prefer each other's good
> from this day forward
> and to love and to cherish
> in sickness and in health
> as long as we may live.

Now we all offer to you (name) and you (name) our sincere good wishes. May you have joy and give joy and make your home a source of strength and happiness to others. I have also been asked to offer you the very best wishes for your future happiness from the Gay and Lesbian Humanist Association. Now you may kiss each other and sign the Affirmation Certificate.

As the ceremony comes to an end the celebrant may think it appropriate to lead those assembled in applause, and it is probably best to ensure that whoever is in charge of the music starts it again at this stage. All parts of the certificate – including the couple's names – should be filled out in advance by the officiant, leaving the couple to sign in the two spaces provided.

⑥

Philip and Steve were keen not to ape heterosexual weddings but used some of their traditional elements to give weight and significance to their ceremony. Both had a best man (who simultaneously handed rings to the officiant), the room was divided into two with an aisle, they read vows and cut a cake. Says Philip, 'We both took the prerogative to arrive late!' After walking down the aisle together, accompanied by music, they stood and faced the congregation.

Introduction by Celebrant

Certain people have tried to narrow down the meaning of 'fam-

ily' so as to exclude anyone who is not married and not heterosexual. This attempt is irritating, but, in the end, meaningless.
We can all create our own family in whatever way we want to.
Our partnerships are labelled as 'pretend' – we know that there
is nothing pretend about the love we can feel for each other, and
nobody can take that away from us.

What Steve and Phil cannot do, as a gay couple, is to have a
wedding ceremony that will have any legal meaning. So they
have invited you, their family and friends, to witness their commitment to each other, to validate their partnership in the eyes
of those who are important to them.

The Affirmation

We have come together to witness the joining together of two
lives. It is the wishes of Steve and Phil that the words of the next
song are listened to, as they have found a 'long and lasting love'.

Steve and Phil have come here in affection and honour to say
before us that they will henceforth continue to share their home,
and combine in mutual living and responsibility. Love is the
wish of the whole self to unite with one another to the end of
personal completeness. Touched by this love, nature yields
tenderness, togetherness, simplicity, honesty and delight. When
two people honestly and sincerely declare their affection for
each other, they are affirming the precious truth that love is the
foundation of all life – between two people, between friends and
between all humanity.

Now, [addressing the couple] will you join right hands. Do
you aspire to love each other and to live together in a spirit of
tolerance, mutual support and concern for each other's well-
being, sharing your responsibilities, your problems and your
joys?

Steve and Phil   Yes, we do.

I now ask you both to speak in truth to each other and to repeat
in the spirit of faithful engagement these words of solemn dec-

laration that voluntarily bind you together.

Will you, Steve, say after me:

> I want it to be known
> that I Steve
> take you Phil
> to be my love
> and promising to cherish
> love and comfort you
> for all my life
> I offer you this ring
> as a symbol of my love.

Will you, Phil, say after me:

> I want it to be known
> that I Phil
> take you Steve
> to be my love
> and promising to cherish
> love and comfort you
> for all my life
> I offer you this ring
> as a symbol of my love.

Now the two of you, together, repeat after me these words:

> We have openly declared our love for each other
> and do pledge ourselves
> to prefer each other's good
> from this day forward
> and to love and to cherish
> in sickness and in health
> as long as we may live.

And now may we offer to you, Steve and Phil, our sincere good wishes. May you have joy and give joy and make your home a source of strength and happiness to yourselves and to others. You may now kiss each other.

Philip says of the ceremony, 'Many were moved to tears. Several gay friends stated afterwards that it had changed their perpective on life.'

Of course, you don't have to follow this formula. *Martin and Roy* held a celebration of partnership after doing some research with the Humanists, Quakers and Spiritualists and, when they were in San Francisco, went along to the county hall and acquired a Declaration of Domestic Partnership. Their ceremony, held in the Forest of Dean, was conducted by a straight couple. As Martin said,

> We wanted someone close to us to conduct the ceremony, rather than an unknown person recommended by an official body. We thought of doing it ourselves, but thought it would be a bit like trying to chair a meeting and take minutes at the same time.

After prayers and readings, their vows were as follows:

Roy   Martin, I promise you my love and commitment, an ear for your joys, a shoulder for your tears and my arms for you always, in all things. I ask you to stand by my side, my partner and lover always. As a token of this bond I give you this ring, for as a ring has no end, so my love for you has no end.

Martin   Roy, I promise to love and comfort you, to listen and hear you and to hold and care for you. I ask you to accept my commitment to you and be with me now, and always. As a token of this bond I give you this ring, for as a ring has no end, so my love for you has no end.

⑥

Amanda and Avril (32, a professional organizer, and 37, a psychotherapist) held a commitment ceremony in a garden. They wrote it themselves, using some material from Becky Butler's book, *Ceremonies of the Heart* (Seal Press, 1990). They also incorporated several ancient traditions: some Pagan, some Goddess, some Jewish and some Buddhist.

Avril and Amanda were led into the circle of guests standing under an apple tree. A friend followed, holding two rings on a velvet cushion.

The ceremony started with an invocation to the Four Elements, read by four friends:

1) East – the Element of Air, linked to the dawn and the masculine qualities of thought and mind.
2) South – the Element of Fire, linked to the noon and the masculine qualities of spirit, will, sexuality and home.
3) West – the Element of Water, linked to the sunset and the feminine qualities of blood, water in the womb, tears and emotions.
4) North – the Element of Earth, linked to midnight and the feminine qualities of silence, wisdom, under the mountains.

This was followed by the convocation, in which the priestess called upon the Goddess and the centre of the circle.

She then welcomed the gathered assembly and outlined the ceremony. Anointing the brides' foreheads with calming essential oils to purify them from fears and anxiety, she led two minutes 'grounding' silence.

The priestess blessed the wine and the bread (two wedding buns) in Hebrew and English.

Another friend stepped forward to explain the next (Buddhist-inspired) ritual, the exchange of white silk scarves, a symbol of white light, love and compassion.

Next, poems were read and the rings blessed by a gay friend, who explained the significance of the rings – an outer symbol of inner commitment.

Avril and Amanda then exchanged their vows, each holding the ring cushion:

I bring myself and my uniqueness to our relationship and I love you for who you are.

I promise to follow my heart and be myself – even if it means going into conflict with you.

I pledge my goodwill to work through conflict or difficulties between us and to get support from others when necessary.

I promise to be open to my own growth and development and to support you in yours.

I commit myself to a monogamous sexual relationship with you.

I promise to make time for myself to nourish my creativity and aliveness and to respect your needs for time alone and with others.

I promise to set aside time to be with you when we can be playful, passionate, sexual and loving.

I look forward to raising a family with you in our safe and loving home.

The priestess went on to explain the glass breaking ritual (*see* page 87), and then everyone gathered around the couple for the final blessing, placing their hands on the shoulders of the people in front to form a silent, loving circle.

This was followed by songs, appreciations and memories from the guests, a toast and chollah (Jewish milk-based bread), before the circle was finally broken, with thanks to the Four Elements.

PAGAN

Lee and Karen also chose a Pagan blessing. It was held in a friend's back garden in front of a group of six close female friends, a priestess and several children.

Again, the Four Quarters were important. In the north of the garden they erected an altar, on which they placed three candles, representing themselves and their son, plus a larger candle representing their union, together with their birth stones, water, fire, fruit, flowers and gifts from friends and family unable to be present.

The priestess Tarah began the ceremony by casting a circle in order to consecrate the space. She cleansed the couple with salted water and incense: this helped them move into the circle unburdened by their everyday lives, and to focus wholly on the rite of union which was about to take place.

The friends stood in the circle, four at the points of the compass representing Air, Fire, Water and Earth (*see* above). Lee was to enter from the East, Karen from the West.

To bring them into the circle, two friends each took a candle from the altar and handed them to the couple. Karen and Lee approached the altar and lit the union candle together.

Tarah began the blessing by recalling when and why Lee and Karen had approached her, she spoke of the blessings they had asked her to give and called upon the Goddess of many guises to be there that day to witness and bless this rite of union.

At this, Karen and Lee walked around the circle from the East to the North, receiving gifts and a blessing from each friend chosen as guardians of the Elements. From the East came an image of a bird (Air); from the South some candles (Fire); from the West a water vessel (Water); and from the North stones (Earth). Each spoke this blessing on offering the gift:

I the Guardian of Air/Fire/Water/Earth bestow a blessing upon your union in the name of Air/Fire/Water/Earth and the grace of the Goddess may it be.

This was then followed by readings and blessings read by other friends, and the priestess read a Goddess prayer from *The Spiral Dance* (Starhawk, HarperSanFrancisco, 1974).

Tarah turned to the couple and asked:

Is it the Goddess you seek to bless your union?
Is it the Goddess of many names you would like me to call and
    witness and bless your vows?
Is this your chosen path?

To each of these Karen and Lee answered 'Yes'.

Tarah offered a prayer to the Goddess, then Lee and Karen exchanged whispered vows, having decided that they did not wish to share the intensely private and personal nature of their vows.

Their son Jacob presented the two rings for them to exchange and Karen was crowned with a circlet of roses. They offered wine and cake to each other, saying:

May you never hunger
May you never thirst.

The cake and wine were then passed round for the toast:

To those who were, to those who are and those who will be.
To those who are here and those who wish to be.
Blessed Be.

The couple left through a processional arch made by their friends (who showered them with rice and petals), and then jumped the broomstick.

Karen says, 'Traditionally a Pagan wedding lasts for a year and a day, at which point the couple are blessed again. Although your marriage is a commitment that we feel is to last for all time (Goddess willing), we will be blessed each year, and will renew our vows. We both feel that this is a good way to reaffirm our commitment to each other.'

SEVEN

GETTING MARRIED ABROAD

⑥

HONEYMOON WEDDINGS

While a wedding at home might cost £6,000, a wedding in Paradise could set you back as little as £1,500.

There are as many possibilities for weddings abroad as there are for holidays.

Tropical weddings are becoming increasingly popular, with rock stars and actors helping to spread the word. Few people will not have heard about Pamela Anderson in her white bikini marrying Tommy Lee on a beach in Cancun, Mexico; or Michael Praed and Karen Landau's wedding in a hotel in Barbados; Madonna's to Sean Penn on the edge of a cliff; or Christie Brinkley's to Ricky Taubman, in skis, on top of a mountain in Colorado.

A wedding on a ski slope is the whitest of white weddings, and some tour companies are now organizing these. Indeed tour companies have been quick to respond to the new market in weddings abroad. Kuoni, for example, has an extensive brochure which covers every conceivable question you might have on tropical weddings.

Whether you want to marry on a beach, in a church or on a boat, there are many destinations to choose from: Caribbean islands, Cancun on the coast of Mexico, Kenya, the Seychelles and Mauritius in the Indian Ocean are just some examples.

White, palm-fringed beaches, stunning sunsets, exotic flowers
. . . the appeal is clear. The organization is easy: the tour company or hotel will do it all for you, including the legal for-
malities, and all you need to do is worry about your dress
creasing on the flight over – if you are wearing a dress, that is!

The ceremony itself is very similar to a civil service back
home. It is conducted by a local official who will say prayers
and words of welcome, and may give a homily on marriage.
Some of the words they use can be rather quaint. In Mauritius,
for example, the groom might be exhorted to 'Love your new
bride always and never, ever look upon her as a fleeting
pleasure', while the bride advised, 'And you, sweet lady, must
always be very, very kind to your hero.' (*The Sunday Times*, 12
February 1995) The exact wording varies from country to country, but the vows and declaration of no impediment are essentially the same. You can go just as a couple or bring family and
friends, but you will need two witnesses.

Nicola and Pascal (35, a diplomat), who married in the
Seychelles, had a civil ceremony in the reception area of a large
hotel under a high-vaulted thatched roof. Frangipani and
orchids created an aisle, while lush green plants and the Indian
Ocean provided the backdrop. Nicola's father escorted her
towards Pascal, who then led her up the flower-strewn floor to
a small table where they sat and went through the civil ceremony. Based on English law, the ceremony was conducted in
French, although the couple made their vows in English. 'If the
weather is good it is just so romantic,' writes Nicola, who now
lives in the Seychelles and has seen several couples take their
vows on the beaches. 'We nearly had our wedding on a small
island called L'Islette which you reach by rowing boat, but we
had too many guests to fit the island!' Catherine (38, a solicitor
and trainer) also waxes lyrical over her wedding on a beach
in Hawaii: 'It was spiritual, exotic, beautiful, remote, intimate,
warm and unusual.'

Katy and Peter wanted to separate the legal and religious
elements of marriage. When they got free tickets to the States

(through a special offer) they decided to do the legal 'bit' there, on a beach in Florida.

> The celebration back at home was because we felt other aspects of marriage were important: we wanted to make a public declaration about our relationship and wanted to have a time to celebrate with and include our families and friends.

Check the weather for the time of year, if a sunny day is important. In the Seychelles, for example, sun is guaranteed in September and October; in December to February, however, your photos may be spoilt by heavy monsoon rains! Bear in mind as well that time differences may cause problems in telephoning people back at home and laid-back attitudes delay responses to letters.

If you decide not to use a tour company, you must find out exactly what the hotel will be organizing (legal documentation, flowers, food, photography and so on), and what you need to do yourselves.

You can, of course, go even more alternative than this and hold a ceremony of your own, barefoot and garlanded, in a jungle in Borneo, for example. When you arrive back home, you could simply tie up the legal side at any register office. If you want to go even more exotic and marry in a temple in Bali or on Mount Kilimanjaro, I'm afraid that is beyond the scope of this book. Your best bet is to try the relevant embassy or travel agent.

LAS VEGAS WEDDINGS

One popular style of wedding is the Las Vegas 'quickie' wedding. Acknowledged by many as the world capital of glitz and tack, Las Vegas boasts a plethora of hotels, casinos and chapels. 75,000 couples from around the world get married in Vegas each year, seduced by the relaxed marriage laws and ease with which you can get hitched within a few hours of picking up the phone.

It's the perfect choice for couples who have been inspired by Nick Cage and Sarah Jessica Parker in *Honeymoon in Vegas*, or for those who want to follow in the real-life footsteps of Hollywood stars.

Although you could simply fly there and arrange the wedding by phone very swiftly once you have arrived, you may prefer to organize everything from the UK. Marriage licences are issued 365 days a year for a fee of $35 (about £23), and the courthouse is on the doorstep of several chapels, each with its own particular set-piece charm. If a drive-in doesn't appeal, you can choose from a wide selection which includes a traditional white Victorian-style chapel, an indoor garden chapel or a quaint country chapel – or even a Graceland wedding chapel with an Elvis lookalike minister . . .

Wedding agencies offer a full 'package' including rings, flowers (which you take from a fridge), music (canned), garter (!), limousine, photographer, video, champagne and reception – although you can telephone the chapels and book direct (hotels or *Yellow Pages* will have the numbers). You can choose between a civil and religious service and, if you want to return in ten years' time to renew your vows, this can also be arranged.

Journalist Jules E. Stevenson was married in the Little Chapel of the Flowers by a 'six-foot babe with blonde candyfloss hair and make-up derived from a rainbow summer collection', but does admit that the civil service she chose was surprisingly moving, focusing on friendship and partnership bonding. And let's not forget the economics of a fun Vegas wedding: 'Bear in mind a 17-day trip with wedding, flight and accommodation probably costs less than a third of a traditional wedding on a wet summer day in July.' (*Ms London*, 20 June 1994) Sumita agrees: 'It was exciting and a chance not to be missed. Another major factor was the unbearable thought of relatives and a boring English do!'

Sumita and Stewart (32, a helicopter instructor) married in the Little Church of the West in Las Vegas. They called the Las Vegas tourist board, several freephone numbers and made the decision based on the packages offered and the price. In the end they plumped for the cheapest at $180 (about £120), which included the service, bouquet, buttonholes and photos. The chapel was the one where Cindy Crawford and Richard Gere got married. There was no need to book in advance and according to Sumita, 'It wasn't too tacky, it had elements of a traditional wedding, and it was over in 10 minutes!'

After handing over the marriage licence – procured from the courthouse for around $35 (about £23) – they were greeted by the minister and presented with a bouquet. The bride and groom marched down the aisle accompanied by an instrumental version of the Righteous Brothers' *Unchained Melody*. 'We didn't choose it,' insists Sumita, 'and it made me giggle as it was the music from *Ghost*!'

This is the service they chose:

Sumita and Stewart, you have come here today to celebrate the love you have for each other. We share in this with you by giving social recognition of your decision to accept each other as husband and wife. Into this state of marriage you have come to be united.

In man's long history he has never discovered a better way of life than sharing it together in love with another in a lasting and responsible way. This arrangement seems to meet our deepest human needs for love and companionship for someone with whom we can share in an intimate and trusting way all the hopes and joys and dreams of life.

Real love, Sumita and Stewart, is something beyond the warmth and glow, the excitement and romance of being deeply in love. It is caring as much about the welfare and happiness of your marriage partner as about your own. But real love is not total absorption into each other, it is looking outward in the same direction together. Love makes burdens lighter, because you divide them. It makes joys more intense, because you share them. It makes you stronger, so you can reach out and become involved with life in ways you dared not risk alone.

Stewart, will you take Sumita as your wife, will you be faithful to her in tender love and honour, offering her encouragement and companionship, and will you live with her and cherish her as love and respect would lead you, in the bond of marriage?

Stewart   I will.

Sumita, will you take Stewart as your husband, will you be faithful to him in tender love and honour, offering him encouragement and companionship, and will you live with him and cherish him as love and respect would lead you, in the bond of marriage?

Sumita   I will.

May I have the rings please? [an attendant hands over the rings]
Sumita and Stewart, as these circles are designed without an ending, they speak of eternity. May the incorruptible substance of these rings represent a love glowing with increasing lustre through the years.

May the Lord God bless these rings which you give to each other as the sign of your love, trust and faithfulness.

Stewart, place the ring on her finger and say to her these words:

This ring I give you in token of my devotion and love. And with my heart I pledge to you all that I am. With this ring I marry you, and join my life to yours.

Sumita, place the ring on his finger and say to her these words:

This ring I give you in token of my devotion and love. And with my heart I pledge to you all that I am. With this ring I marry you, and join my life to yours.

And now share with me this brief prayer:

O God, look graciously upon this couple as they share life together, its struggles and problems as well as the joys and blessings, that, in the experiences of life, they will stay close to each other.
Amen.

Sumita and Stewart, you have here promised to share your lives in marriage in the presence of God, friends and family. Therefore I now acknowledge that you are husband and wife.

OTHER WEDDINGS ABROAD

One thing couples who get married abroad often forget is that their wedding will be in a foreign language. If this does not bother you and you thrill to the idea of simply saying *si* to an official – go ahead! People I spoke to said it was fantastically spontaneous and great fun.

Not by any stretch of the imagination a quickie wedding, the marriage of *Jeanette and Jim* (26, a drama worker, and 31, unemployed) in Prague Town Hall took six months to arrange. On arrival they were led to a room where an official checked their documents and gave them an eclectic list of music to choose from. Apparently an organist was on hand to play whatever took their fancy, from The Beatles to Verdi. In the end they chose a piece by Smetana for the entrance, *Rhapsody in Blue* by Gershwin for the exchange of rings and Verdi's 'Gloria All'Egitto' for their exit.

They proceeded in pairs, Jim on his mother's arm, Jeanette on her father's, to a large table in the grand, bright town hall. The ceremony was read out first in Czech, then in English. The only participation required of Jim and Jeanette was to state that they had come 'voluntarily and of our own free will'. After the exchange of rings the translator piped up: 'And now the first nuptial kiss, please.' The mayoress shook their hands and congratulated them, another official offered them champagne and gave them the cork for luck. The following day the couple returned to collect their marriage certificate.

This is a translation of Jeanette and Jim's ceremony, handed to them on the day.

Dear engaged couple, heartily welcome in this lovely, old town hall, where you have come, accompanied by your relatives and friends, to have your decision to live together as husband and wife solemnized.

You are standing here on the loveliest day of your life, which cannot be repeated again, full of love and ideas about your future and faith in the fact that your marriage bond will surpass all troubles and problems.

I wish you from my full heart that this faith and trust may accompany you at all common occasions, even if they are unpleasant, which sometimes may be the case. That is why I also wish you, besides the mutual love, above all mutual understanding, trust and tolerance. You leave your hitherto background and new friendships and relationships will take place.

Now you must build up your new family, sharing common aims. But your ideas and their realization may differ sometimes. At any misunderstanding which may come about, remember this solemn day and all hopes related to it.

Your solemn promise of today not only combines your lives, but is also the origin of the children which you will have together. Build up for them something that cannot be bought with any money, the only thing that cannot be replaced by anything other – a harmonious home full of love and understanding. Teach your children to look for pleasure in their lives and to respect higher spiritual values. Give them faith in goodness and hope, in the same way as your parents have handed it over to you today.

This is mainly your day, the day with the capital 'D', but in spite of this, remember just now your parents. Pay them in your minds words of thanks for their love to you, as well as words of gratitude, because they sacrificed for you all that was theirs. Thank them for trying to teach you the best they could and to hand over a piece of their hearts to you. They know that you will be in need of them even in the future and they are ready to help you.

They know – as you will find out with your own children – that there is nothing more important for a parent, besides God, than the health and happiness of their children, at whose bed-side they once sat (and not so long ago), comforting during times of illness and feeling such pleasure when their efforts helped.

Today they have accompanied you here that they may bless your new way of life. And now I may only add a short extract from one of the nicest songs of Jaques Brell:

> Come my love, a lucky chance is my shield
> and my love will be on guard,
> as you are the creature for which I am long sick . . .
> Just now the time is coming for us to love and to live,
> come with me to look for our island – there, far off.

Be happy together and God save you and your marriage bond!

EIGHT

A FINAL
WORD OF ADVICE

I asked the alternative couples who contributed to this book to offer some advice to other couples contemplating breaking from tradition and 'doing it their way'. No one I spoke to had any regrets and their words are printed here, as a postscript to the book. May they give you encouragement to follow your own convictions!

It is *your* wedding: do what *you* want.

Be careful how vulnerable you make yourself if lots of people are going to be there.

Say right from the beginning that you are going to do something different and keep saying it.

Follow your heart. Ours was the most beautiful day – many people said it changed their lives. It inspired people to rethink how they would marry.

Consider explaining the background to the wedding to those present. Find some way of making your guests at ease with the ceremony you offer as they would be with one that they know.

Take advantage of the fact that you have total choice over where, when and how the ceremony is carried out to create an event that is cohesive, that doesn't break in the middle between ceremony and reception because the church is in one place and the 'reception' in another. That way, the whole gathering of people, being together for the ceremony and then the celebration, can be one total event and hence more memorable.

Give yourself a long honeymoon; if any kind of wedding is tiring, one where you are so much more in charge of the ceremony and its impact is four times as nerve-wracking and exhausting.

Be sure that it is what you want and the ceremony feels right. Allow others to control the bits they want to.

Make enough time and space to think about the ceremony and vows you really want. Try not to be dominated by your parents.

Expensive or cheap, the most wonderful thing about marriage is the love and commitment to each other you are making.

Do it! Do it your own way, make it your own day that's special to you and your relationship. Don't listen to people who say 'it can't be done'.

If you have problems with parents, keep calm, try to reason with them, but remember it's YOUR wedding, not theirs.

Make sure that your principles are upheld, but compromise if you have to in order to keep the peace. My parents were pleased we at least had our reception in a church hall.

If you discuss your feelings with your parents tactfully, you will find that they will respect your choice of wedding.

Don't feel pressurized by society to have a church wedding. There are so many other more exciting and cheaper ways to do it.

If you're going to have an outdoor ceremony, beware rain and wind carrying your words away.

Don't go for anything too risky or too wacky. The wedding has to be a meaningful ritual for you and for your guests, otherwise you won't feel married. And if you do too much that is risky – helicopter weddings, etc. – then your mind will be on that and not on each other.

If you choose to get married on a Sunday, it will be easier to book musicians, caterers and the reception venue. But remember that people may have to leave early and not want to sing and dance late into the night.

Don't let family or friends persuade you out of it. You will never forgive yourself if you compromise. Instead, get everyone involved with something to do – they'll forget to fight you over the ceremony and will feel part of it.

Follow your heart and have the wedding you always dreamed of, not what others want or expect or what the law states. You are making the commitment; no one else is.

In a sense it is a portrait of who you are, who you have been and who you will be in the future. So make sure it is authentically *you*.

Go ahead and do it, make a stand. It is your life and you should be able to make your feelings and love and commitment known. Above all be positive and believe in what you are doing and why.

I hope this book has helped you to plan a unique wedding day. I have a private theory, completely unsubstantiated by official statistics, that despite the high divorce rates, an alternative wedding – where you are really putting your heart and soul into the words you are saying, the music and the readings – has a far higher chance of succeeding than a marriage where the couple values convention and tradition above content and feeling.

I wish you all the happiness in the world.

PLANNING CHECKLIST

Use this as a working chart to fill in your own details and to check progress.

Location	
Date	
Time	
Celebrant (minister, priest, rabbi, registrar)	
Special licence	
Notice given to register office	
Documents needed	
Attendants/participants	
Guest list	
Wedding present list	
Clothes	

Rings	
Transport to/from wedding	
Photographer/video	
Invitations	
Service sheets	
Music	
Flowers	
Cake	
Catering	
Table plan	
Gifts for each other/attendants	
Honeymoon	

USEFUL ADDRESSES

Baptists Union
Baptist House
129 The Broadway
Didcot
Oxon OX11 8RT
01235 512077

British Humanist Association
47 Theobald's Road
London WC1X 8SP
0171 4300908

Buddhist Society
58 Eccleston Square
London SW1
0171 8345858

The Catholic Marriage Advisory
  Council
Clitherow House
1 Blythe Mews
Blythe Road
London W14 0NW
0171 3711341

Central Register Office for
  Northern Ireland
Oxford House
49–55 Chichester Street
Belfast BT1 4HL
01232 250000

Church of Scotland Department
  of Communication
Wesley Owens Books
117 George Street
Edinburgh EH4 2JN
0131 2252229

Churches Conservation Trust
89 Fleet Street
London EC4Y 1DH
0171 9362285

Gay and Lesbian Humanist
  Association
34 Spring Lane
Kenilworth
Warwickshire DV8 2HB
01926 58450

General Register Office for
  Scotland
New Register House
Edinburgh EH1 3YT
0131 3144447

General Synod of the Church of
  England
Church House
Great Smith Street
London SW1P 3NZ
0171 2229011

Jewish Marriage Council
23 Ravenshurst Avenue
London NW4 4EE
0181 2036311

Lesbian and Gay Christian
  Movement
Oxford House
Derbyshire Street
London E2 6HG
0171 5871235

London Baha'i Centre
27 Rutland Gate
London SW7
0171 5840843
01279 816363

Methodist Church
Westminster Central Hall
Storey's Gate
London SW1 9NH
0171 2228010

Quakers Religious Society of
  Friends
Friends House
173–177 Euston Road
London NW1
0171 3873601

Redundant Churches
Church Commissioners
1 Millbank
Westminster
SW1P 3JZ
0171 2227010

Register General for England
  and Wales
Smedley Hydro
Trafalgar Road
Southport
Merseyside PR8 2HH
0151 4714200

Register General for Guernsey
The Greffe
Royal Court House
St Peter Port
Guernsey GY1 2PB
01481 725277

Superintendent Register for
  Jersey
States Buildings
10 Royal Square
St Helier
Jersey JE1 IDD
01534 502000

The Unitarian and Free Christian
  Churches
Central Administration Office
Essex Hall
1–6 Essex St
London WC2R 3HY
0171 2402384

United Reformed Church
86 Tavistock Place
London WC1H 9RT
0171 9162020

HOLIDAY/WEDDINGS

**Afro-Caribbean Wedding and
Events Planner** (0181 6566865)
Airtours (01706 830130)
Las Vegas, Antigua, Barbados,
Jamaica, Grand Camna,
Florida, Austria, Cyprus,
Kenya, Los Angeles,
San Francisco.
Airwaves (0181 8751188)
Thailand, Seychelles,
Mauritius, Hong Kong, Fiji,
Barbados, St Lucia, Granada,
Antigua, South Africa.

**Australian Tourist
Commission** (0181 7802227)
Provide a useful fact sheet.
BA Holidays (01293 517555)
Antigua, St Lucia, Barbados,
Jamaica, Seychelles, Mauritius,
Bali, Sri Lanka, Kenya, Fiji.
Caribbean Connection (01244
341131)
Anguilla, Antigua, Barbuda,
Bahamas, Barbados, Bermuda,
Cayman Islands, Florida,
Grenada, Jamaica, Monserrat,
St Lucia, St Kitts, St Vincent
and the Grenadines, Trinidad
and Tobago, Turks and Caicos
Islands, Virgin Islands.
Caribtours (0171 5813517)
Jamaica, Barbados, St Lucia,
St Kitts, Grenada, Antigua,
St Vincent and the Grenadines.
Elegant Resorts (01244 329671)
Barbados, Grenada, Jamaica,
St Lucia, Antigua, Anguilla,
Young Island (Grenadines),
British Virgin Islands,
Bermuda, Mauritius,
Seychelles, Malaysia, Fiji, Cook
Islands, Hawaii, Hayman
Island (Australia).
Inspirations (01293 820207)
India, Sri Lanka, Kenya, Crete,
Cyprus.
Kuoni (01306 742222)
Seychelles, Mauritius, Kenya,
Bali, Australia, Fiji, Florida,

Bahamas, Hawaii, Antigua,
St Kitts, Grenada, Jamaica,
St Lucia, Barbados, Malaysia.
Silk Cut Travel (0130 265211)
St Lucia, Antigua, Barbados,
Grenada, St Kitts, Anguilla,
Seychelles, Mauritius,
Thailand, Malaysia and Bali.
Somak (0181– 4233000)
Kenya, Mauritius, Seychelles.
Thomas Cook (01733 – 332255)
Mauritius, Seychelles, Kenya,
Bermuda, Grenada, St Lucia,
Barbados, Antigua, Jamaica,
Bali, Penang, Thailand.
Thompson (0171 3879321)
St Lucia, Antigua, Barbados,
Dominican Republic, Grenada,
Jamaica, Kenya, Mauritius,
Mexico, the Seychelles and
St Kitts-Nevis.
Tradewinds (01706 232316)
Thailand, Malaysia, Bali, Sri
Lanka, Seychelles, Mauritius,
Hawaii, Florida, Fiji, Antigua,
St Lucia, Tobago, Bahamas,
Granada.
Unijet (01444 459191)
St Lucia, Barbados, Grenada,
Antigua, Jamaica.
Virgin Holidays (01293
617181)
Florida, Miami, Orlando,
St Pete's, Sarasota, Clearwater,
Key Largo, Bahamas, Jamaica,
Las Vegas, Lake Tahoe,

Vermont.
Virgin Snow Weddings (01273
744265)

FIREWORKS

The Firework Company
Shine House
High Street
Uffculme
Devon EX15 3AB
01884 840504

LAS VEGAS

Las Vegas Wedding Agency
2595 Chandler Avenue 14
Las Vegas NV 89120
USA
001 702 7364255

RING DESIGNERS

Nick Kellet
68 New Kings Road
London SW6 4LT
0171 7363258

Nichola Fletcher
Reediehill Farm
Auchtermuchty
Fife
Scotland KY14 7HS
01337 828369

Elizabeth Gage
20 Albemarle St
London W1
0171 4992879

NON-RELIGIOUS
WEDDINGS SPECIALIST

Linda Thurlow
Garlands
25 Highfield Road
Maidenhead
Berkshire SL6 5DF
01628 26852

STATIONERY
WITH A DIFFERENCE

East Coast Design
4 East Avenue
Whitley Bay
Northumberland NE25 8EJ
0191 2515432

Illustrated Stationery Ltd
Ty-rhiw Estate
Taffs Well
South Wales CF4 7RZ
01222 811024

Nick Townsend Calligraphy
Flat 3, Hazelbury House
Draycott Terrace
St Ives
Cornwall TR26 2EF
01736 797825

TRANSPORT

American Wedding Cars
77 Tallis Way
Borehamwood
Hertfordshire WD6 4TQ
0181 9532911

CB Helicopters
Westland Heliport
Lombard Road
London SW11
0171 2283232

Head in the Clouds
(Hot-air balloons)
Sprats Hatch Farm
Dogmersfield
Basingstoke
Hampshire RG27 8TH
01252 617616

UNUSUAL DRESS DESIGNS

Rebecca Street
The Alternative Wedding Shop
294 Upper Street
Islington
London N1 2TU
0171 3549955

POSTER SITES

Adshel
33 Golden Square
London W1R 3PA
0171 2876100

FURTHER READING

Ceremonies of the Heart, Becky Butler (Seal Press, 1990).

Circles of Love, Rabbi Dr Rudy Brasch (HarperCollins Australia, 1995).

Daring to Speak Love's Name, Elizabeth Stewart (Heinemann).

The Druid Way, Philip Carr Gomm (Element, 1993).

Emily Post on Second Weddings, Elizabeth L. Post (HarperPerennial, 1991).

Great Occasions, ed. Andrew Hill (General Assembly of Unitarian Churches, 1992).

Humanism, The Great Human Detective Story (a video available from the BHA).

Marriage: A fortress for well-being (The Baha'i Publishing Trust, 1973, 1988).

Marriage of Likeness: same sex unions in pre-modern Europe, John Boswell (HarperCollins, 1995).

Thompson's *Weddings in Paradise* (video on tropical weddings).

Together Forever, Andrew Marshall (Cassells, 1995).

To Love and To Cherish, Jane Wynne Willson (British Humanist Association, 1988).

The Two of Us: Affirming, Celebrating and Symbolizing Gay and Lesbian Relationships, Larry J. Uhrig (Alyson Press, 1985).

Weddings from the Heart, Daphne Rose Kingma (Conari Press, 1991).

The Oxford Book of Marriage, Helge Rubenstein (Oxford University Press, 1992).

INDEX